RELATING

WHILE AUTISTIC

Fixed Signals for Neurodivergent Couples

Wendela Whitcomb Marsh, MA, RSD

RELATING WHILE AUTISTIC
Fixed Signals for Neurodivergent Couples

All marketing and publishing rights guaranteed to and reserved by:

FUTURE HORIZONS

(817) 277-0727

(817) 277-2270 (fax)

E-mail: info@fhautism.com

www.fhautism.com

ISBN: 9781957984049

Contents

Relating While Autistic

— PART II —

Contents

Relating While Autistic

Contents

— PART IV —

Introduction

All Aboard!

Turn Mixed Signals into Fixed Signals

"The concept of neurodiversity provides a paradigm shift in how we think... Instead of... deficit, disease, or dysfunction... neurodiversity suggests that we instead speak about differences..."

— Dr. Thomas Armstrong, *The Power of Neurodiversity*

Introduction: All Aboard!

Neurodivergent (ND) couples, wherein one or both partners have autism spectrum disorder (ASD), attention-deficit/hyperactivity disorder (ADHD), or another brain difference, often struggle with mixed signals. He said one thing, she heard something else, and they both jumped to conclusions about what their partner really meant.

Autism includes challenges to social communication, and nowhere is social communication more important than in a marriage or committed relationship.

If you're holding this book now, you may be in an ND relationship, wondering why it seems so hard to communicate with the one you love.

Maybe you're not in a relationship yet, and you know you need some solid communication skills in place before you find the right one so you can make it work.

Perhaps you're a counselor or therapist who works with couples, and your ND clients have unique needs and don't respond to your tried-and-true strategies the way your neurotypical (NT) couples do.

You might be an NT with an ND couple among your family or friends, and you want to better understand them.

One thing ND couples have in common is a propensity to have mixed signals, yearning to communicate clearly and effectively but finding that desire thwarted time and time again.

Relating While Autistic

Whatever your reason for being here, the important question is: How can ND couples turn mixed signals into fixed signals?

You've come to the right place.

In this book you'll find practical tips, evidence-based strategies, and the keys couples need to unlock their best relationship.

It's built on the science of human behavior, relationship research, and what I've learned from my own twenty-seven years in love as part of a brilliant, powerful, and magical ND marriage.

The most important thing to remember on your journey to understanding as a couple is that solutions to problems are never on the shoulders of just one of you.

If you think the ND partner should make all of the changes and try to be more like the majority in an NT society, you are wrong. ND individuals have a right to be as quirky as they like, within legal and moral limits, of course.

If you believe that the NT partner should make all of the changes because they do not have a "handicap" and their partner does, you are wrong there, too. ND people are able to learn, grow, and change their own behaviors just as NT people are.

This cannot be a one-sided journey. There may be certain things which are non-negotiable for either one of you, and you each need to learn to become aware of your partner's needs, but never at the expense of your own needs. When two people love each other, as you do, you can always work toward the middle

Introduction: All Aboard!

ground, where everyone gets their needs met and no one carries the entire burden of change.

You are your partner's beloved, and they are yours. You love one another, and you can learn together what each of you needs and how you can meet those needs.

You're probably already doing that in many ways.

I know it's not easy, but I also know it's possible. Your relationship is worth the work you'll put in to make it strong and successful.

One way we'll be exploring relationship mixed signals in this book is through *Red Light/Green Light Tips* that demonstrate what not to do or say, with more effective things to try instead.

What Shall We Talk About? conversation starters for Family Meetings open the gates to your own discussions about what's important to the two of you.

There will be *Date Night Themes* offering ideas for planned date nights to keep the love light burning.

Another way we'll learn to turn mixed signals into fixed signals is through four *Fictional Couples Fixing Mixed Signals*. One or both partners in each couple is ND, with characteristics associated with ASD or ADHD. Reading about how they deal with miscommunication and misunderstandings can help other couples on a similar journey. They really are fictional, so any resemblance to real people is entirely coincidental and unintended.

Relating While Autistic

Finally, each chapter ends with *They Say*, stories shared by ND couples about what has worked in their relationships.

 RED LIGHT/GREEN LIGHT TIPS

 RED LIGHT: **You and your partner keep getting mixed signals, you both think you're right, and you worry that the misunderstandings will hurt your relationship.**

 Green Lights:

- Do listen to your partner with love and respect, even if you have a different perspective. Remember, each person experiences the same event through their own lens, and you can both be right about how you remember it. If you feel an interruption or disagreement bubbling up inside you, try doing something physical to keep yourself in check. For instance, put a hand over your mouth or a finger to your lips, or hold an object that will remind you, such as a smooth stone. You could even write the word "wait" or "shh" on the stone with a marker.

Introduction: All Aboard!

○ Do listen and accept your partner's memory of a shared event, rather than interrupting to tell it "right." This can feel like gaslighting.

WHAT SHALL WE TALK ABOUT?

Family Meeting Discussion Opener

Take turns telling each other your memories of the first time you two met or when you first knew you liked each other. What was your favorite part of your first date? What made you smile?

DATE NIGHT THEME

First Date

Try to recreate your first date in some way. This does not have to be literal; it may not be possible to go to the same restaurant or event. If you saw a movie on your first date, maybe you can stream it on TV, cuddling under a blanket and sharing a bowl of popcorn. It's not important to do the exact same things you did, but do remember the feelings of those early days of falling in love.

Relating While Autistic

FICTIONAL COUPLES FIXING MIXED SIGNALS

Let me introduce you to four fictional couples. Some partners are NeuroDivergent (ND) and some are NeuroTypical (NT). You may remember Trish (ND) & Bill (ND) from *Dating While Autistic* (W. Marsh, 2023.) You'll also meet Justin (ND) & Maggie (NT), Lucia (ND) & Naima (ND), and Crow (NT) & Daisy (ND). Throughout the book we'll see how they met various challenges and kept their love on track.

Trish & Bill

Trish and Bill met when they were in their early thirties at a lecture series on the history of science fiction, a shared interest. They took their relationship very slowly from friendship to dating, and were mutually surprised to learn that they were both autistic. They got along so well and felt so comfortable in one another's company, a new experience for both of them, that it seemed inevitable that they would fall in love.

And that's exactly what they did.

Justin & Maggie

Justin and Maggie met in college where they were IT students. They both minored in drama for fun and were cast opposite each other often enough that they became close. Maggie loved Justin's quirky

Introduction: All Aboard!

sense of humor and off-the-wall comments. They often carried on entire conversations using quotes from plays they'd been in or TV shows they binged together. They moved in together after graduation, got jobs in tech, and settled into a routine. Unfortunately, as time went by, they found themselves stuck in a rut, arguing about the same things over and over. One day Justin ended up walking away because, as usual, he couldn't seem to get his ideas across. The arguments made him feel like he was going to explode. He sat in his car trying to calm down, scrolling through his phone, and watching random videos. Suddenly he leaned forward and put his face close to the screen, then replayed the TikTok he'd just seen several times, followed by other similar ones. Eventually he went back inside, handed his phone to Maggie, and said, "I think I'm autistic. Just like this TikToker." Maggie started to laugh, until she saw how serious he looked. She watched the video in wonder as she recognized so many traits Justin shared.

Finally she said, "Yeah, I think maybe you are."

That's where their journey into understanding began.

Lucia & Naima

Lucia and Naima had been true crime fans since they were girls. Back then it was weird to be interested in serial killers and watch CSI shows instead of cartoons. As they grew up, they found others who shared their interests, Lucia at Whittier College and Naima

Relating While Autistic

across the country at Howard University. After graduation they found it hard to connect with people and make friends. The two of them met in an online true crime discussion forum and hit it off. When Lucia mentioned that she was looking forward to the next episode of *Supernatural*, she found out Naima was binge-watching it, too. Another day Naima said how excited she was to get a package in the mail, not just for the item she had ordered, but for the bubble wrap she expected to find. Popping the bubble wrap was to be her weekend treat. Lucia got it and showed her the popping fidget she loved, providing a never-ending bubble wrap pop-fest. They were delighted to keep finding things they had in common.

Eventually, when Naima's job went 100% online and she could work remotely anywhere, she moved across the country to be with Lucia. They fell in love and planned their perfect wedding, small and quiet.

Lucia mentioned that, of course, the wedding would have to be "autism friendly."

Naima didn't understand.

"You know, because we're autistic, we'll we want a reception with a sensory room, and safe, familiar foods. Stuff like that."

"Whoa, whoa, whoa. What do you mean, *we're autistic*?!"

"Uh, what do you mean, what do I mean?"

"We're not autistic, Lucia. I don't know why you would say such a thing."

Introduction: All Aboard!

"Well, I'm certainly autistic. I assumed you were, too. Just about everyone on the site where we met is neurodivergent in one way or another."

Naima had to take a break from this conversation. She went to her room, wrapped herself up in the blanket she'd had her whole life, and rocked gently back and forth while rubbing the frayed satin binding.

After a while Lucia came and sat beside her, rocking in the same rhythm but not speaking or touching her. Several minutes later Naima was ready to talk.

"Why do you think you're autistic? You don't look autistic or anything."

"I don't 'think' I am; I know I'm autistic. And what are autists supposed to look like, anyway? I've always been awkward in social situations. I can't stand to look at people's eyes or listen to them chewing. I feel better when I can spend a lot of time alone every day to recharge my batteries."

"But everybody feels that way about things, right?" Naima knew she did.

Lucia shook her head. "No, not everybody. Neurotypical people don't even think about how long to hold eye contact, or wonder which facial expression they're supposed to put on, or plan out what they're going to say in advance for every conversation. Those are things autistic people do all the time. Anyway,

Relating While Autistic

I got diagnosed years ago, before I met you, so it's not up for discussion. You're engaged to an autist. Surprise!"

"Okay, okay, so you know you're autistic. But not me. I'm just your typical blerd."

"Blerd?" Lucia asked.

"Yeah, black nerd. Why would you think I'm autistic?"

"Well, look at yourself." Naima stopped rocking and rubbing her blanket and clasped her hands tightly together in embarrassment.

"Hey, if it makes me feel better when I'm stressed out, why shouldn't I have a blanket? There's nothing wrong with it."

"Of course there's nothing wrong with it." Lucia bumped her shoulder gently against Naima's. "There's nothing wrong with being autistic, either."

"OMG, Lucia! I didn't mean to say there's anything wrong with you! I love you, exactly as you are. You're perfect! I'm just … surprised. And I've never liked surprises."

"Me neither. It's one of my autistic traits."

The two talked for hours into the night, and Lucia shared blogs, videos, and books about autism. Eventually Naima realized that she, too, was neurodivergent, and most likely on the autism spectrum. It was quite a revelation. It would take her some time exploring and learning before she would consider seeking a diagnosis. For now, self-diagnosis was good enough for her.

Introduction: All Aboard!

Daisy & Crow

Daisy is an autistic cisgender woman (pronouns she/her), and Crow is neurotypical (NT) and nonbinary (pronouns they/theirs). The two met in a Dungeons and Dragons (D&D) game at their local comic book store. Daisy was intrigued by Crow's short purple hair, multiple piercings, and colorful tattoos. She had so many questions! One day they were waiting at the bus stop after D&D, and she saw her chance.

DAISY: Did it hurt to get all those tattoos?

CROW: Yeah, some, but it wasn't bad.

DAISY: Do you have any more tattoos that I can't see?

CROW: If I do, and you can't see them, then they're none of your business.

DAISY: What kind of a name is Crow?

CROW: It's my name.

DAISY: I never heard it before. Is it a man's name or a woman's name?

CROW: It's just a name.

DAISY: The thing is, I can't tell if you're a man or a woman.

CROW: I get that a lot.

DAISY: So, are you a man or a woman?

CROW: No.

DAISY: Did you have surgery to cut off your penis or to sew on a penis?

Relating While Autistic

CROW: None of your business. And I'm not trans, I'm nonbinary. And it's still none of your business. Change the subject.

DAISY: Okay. What's nonbinary?

CROW: That's not changing the subject.

DAISY: I didn't say "penis." And how will I learn if I don't ask?

CROW: Google it. Nobody wants to answer a bunch of personal questions. It's rude and annoying.

DAISY: Yeah, I get that a lot. I can't help but notice that you're not asking me any questions.

CROW: Maybe there's nothing I want to know about you.

DAISY: "My age is 1000, and my gender is dragon!"

CROW: ...What?

DAISY: You didn't ask, so I told you. Actually I got that line online—line online, get it?

CROW: It's not a joke; it's just two words that sound alike.

DAISY: Anyway, since you didn't ask, I got it from "10 Best Statements Ever Uttered During D&D (That Are Too Hilarious for Words.)."

CROW: That stuff you read on the internet isn't real. It's just click bait.

DAISY: But how am I supposed to know what to say if I don't read it first? And how are we supposed to be friends if I don't talk to you?

CROW: What makes you think we should be friends?

Introduction: All Aboard!

DAISY: Because we're both weird. You're weird on the outside, and I'm weird on the inside, but we're still the same. We should be friends.

CROW: (*Chuckling*) You really are weird, aren't you?

DAISY: That's what I just told you. Didn't you hear me?

CROW: Why do you have to be so annoying?

DAISY: I'm autistic. What's your excuse?

(*A bus pulls up.*)

CROW: This is my bus. (Crow gets on the bus and turns back to Daisy on the bench.) Goodbye, weird autistic girl.

DAISY: Goodbye, weird—what do I call you, weird girl or weird boy?

CROW: (*Shakes their head as the bus doors close*)

THEY SAY

My partner and I met while working as shift managers at Burger King. I think I love most her undeniable love for those she loves. She goes above and beyond for them and has such a caring nature.

— Thomas McDonald III

Relating While Autistic

When I met my husband, we were in the same support group, so we got to know each other at a distance without having many one-on-one conversations. When he finally asked me out, we weren't really strangers, but we hadn't spent time just with each other. I learned in the group that he was honest, intelligent, and thoughtful and the kind of person who would always do what he said he would do. I never heard him say a mean word about anyone.

While we were dating, I learned that he was kind to everyone. You can tell a lot about someone by how they treat waitstaff or homeless people asking for a handout. I really loved his quirky sense of humor, too. I fell in love with him and learned that he'd been in love with me for years before he got the nerve to ask me out. Throughout our marriage, when there were odd miscommunications that were surprising given how smart he was, I just remembered that these issues were small in the context of who I knew him to be and our love for each other.

Later, when our son was diagnosed with Asperger's, things started to fall into place. We both realized that he was on the spectrum, too. It didn't change our love, but it helped, when those odd misunderstandings came up, to realize that this is normal for autism. I could be more patient with him, but more importantly, he could be more forgiving of himself.

— Charlene, NT, married to Scott, ND

Introduction: All Aboard!

We met when I was at work and he came in. I was still getting over my divorce, so I friend-listed him for about two years. Unlike men from my past, he never gave up!

— Wendy B.

PART I

STOP! Mixed Signals

"Successful long-term relationships are created through small words, small gestures, and small acts."

— Dr. John Gottman, author of *Eight Dates*

Chapter 1

Verbal Mixed Signals to Fixed Signals

Not Everyone You Like Will Like You

"When I am under stress, don't ask me questions because it makes it worse."

— CH

Chapter 1: Verbal Mixed Signals to Fixed Signals

Verbal communication issues are a hallmark of autism and a challenge shared by many NDs. It can be stressful, especially if you are trying to have a conversation while there are competing sounds or other sensory experiences. If you need to have a serious conversation, plan to have it in a quiet, familiar place with no distractions. Under extreme stress, an ND might lose their ability to hear and understanding what is being said or may even become unable to speak. Situational mutism, rather than selective mutism, can be the result of stressful situations. The person is not choosing to remain silent or "selecting" mutism, but in the presence of sensory, social, or communication overload, verbal language can be significantly impaired.

Here are some common red light issues surrounding verbal communication that lead to mixed signals, with corresponding green light suggestions for fixing those mixed signals.

 RED LIGHT/GREEN LIGHT TIPS FOR VERBAL COMMUNICATION

 RED LIGHT: Poor Auditory Memory

 Green Lights:

- Do use sticky notes as reminders, placed where they can be easily seen, rather than relying on remembering what you heard.

Relating While Autistic

- Do make lists for things to do, buy, or say. This can include things like complimenting or thanking your partner on a regular basis.
- Do use a phone calendar and set reminders. Choose a ring tone that is not too jarring or aversive.

 RED LIGHT: Difficulty Joining Social Conversations

 Green Lights:

- Do use a visual signal of some kind, even a raised hand, to let others know you've got something to add, especially if you can't tell for sure when it's your turn to talk.
- Do give yourself and your partner permission to just watch and listen rather than joining into social conversations. If this is more comfortable for you, there's no need to feel pressured to talk.

 RED LIGHT: Literal Interpretation of Language

 Green Lights:

- Do be aware if you use language literally but your partner does not, and check for understanding. By the same token, if your partner uses language literally but you do not, be aware of this as well.

Chapter 1: Verbal Mixed Signals to Fixed Signals

- Do remember the person you love has their own language style, and if it's not the same as yours, that's okay. Neither of you should expect your partner to change to match your style.

 RED LIGHT: Becoming Distracted in the Middle of a Conversation

 Green Lights:

- Do use a fidget item to keep your hands busy so you can focus on the speaker if you want to follow the conversation because it's interesting, or because you like the people, or because your partner likes the them and you want to please your partner.

- Don't check your phone, read a book, or play a game even if the conversation is boring. If you really do not want to be part of a particular conversation but you do want to hang out with these people, consider staying in the room but allowing yourself to be mentally distracted. If you decide to hang in with the group, the topic may turn towards something you're more interested in.

- Do create a graceful exit script for yourself. You want to leave without hurting anyone's feelings. Talk to your partner in advance if you think this scenario is likely to come up so they won't feel like you've ditched them. Discuss together how each of you could signal secretly that you want to leave a social group conversation.

 RED LIGHT: Misunderstanding/Being Misunderstood

 Green Lights:

- Do ask for clarification if you're not sure what someone meant by what they said. If you're pretty sure you understand but you're not 100% confident, tell them what you heard and understood, and let them correct you if it wasn't what they meant. When in doubt, find out.

- Do think about how others might interpret your words if you find that people take what you say the wrong way. Remember that humans are emotional and often take things personally. An honest suggestion may be taken as rudeness. They may think you are saying they are a bad parent/spouse/worker, when you were only responding to a concern that they had voiced. Tread softly.

- Do ask if your partner is looking for a solution, a hug, a listening ear, or a shoulder to cry on, so you can avoid misinterpreting their needs.

Chapter 1: Verbal Mixed Signals to Fixed Signals

Do be aware that your partner's needs may be completely different from what you would want in a similar situation, so don't assume you know what they need from you.

 RED LIGHT: Too Many Questions

 Green Lights:

Do wait patiently after you ask a question. Auditory processing can take time.

Do resist the urge to repeat or paraphrase your question. Your partner may be processing your words and planning how to respond. If you paraphrase it, they may think you're asking a new question each time and try to process each one as separate but simultaneous questions. This is stressful.

Do let your partner know how you feel if questions make you anxious. Chances are they have no idea you feel that way. Once they know, they can try to ask fewer questions.

Do take some time out and back off if you see that your partner froze or became uncommunicative after you asked them something, rather than continuing to talk. Stop using verbal language, and either wait in silence, reschedule the conversation for a less stressful time, or write them a note about it instead of relying on verbal communication alone.

- Do let your partner know if you heard the question but can't respond to it in the moment. If you can't put it into words, hold up a finger or find another way to let them know you're thinking about it. If you can't handle the discussion at all right now, ask to schedule a time to talk about it when you are better able to focus.
- Do ask them how they would prefer to field questions, in writing or verbally. Be sure to choose a calm, unstressful time to ask this.
- Do ask for a time-out if you get overwhelmed because your partner asks you multiple questions. They may be trying to clarify or be helpful. They mean well, but they don't understand that more questions equals more stress. You can get back to the question later, either in writing or by bringing up the topic again when you're ready to talk.

Chapter 1: Verbal Mixed Signals to Fixed Signals

 RED LIGHT: Situational Mutism

 Green Lights:

- Do have a nonverbal signal to let your partner know when a stressful situation robs you of your ability to speak. It might be making a "T" with your hands for "Time Out" or anything that works for you, as long as you both know the signal.
- Do stop the discussion as soon as your partner gives the "Time Out" signal. Resist the urge to get in the last word. The outcome will be better if you wait for another time when you're both calmer, so stop talking and walk away. Of course, if the two of you are in a public place, don't walk away and ditch them, but help them make a graceful exit.
- Do consider writing letters or notes about things that are important to share but difficult to say. Always start and end each one with honest words of love, affirmation, compliments, things that you adore about your partner, things you are grateful for in them. Then carefully word the middle of the letter, especially if it might cause offense. You want your loving desire to come to an agreement to shine through the tough topic. After addressing the issue of concern, close with more

loving words from your heart. If your partner gives you a letter like this, resist the impulse to gloss over the positive statements and fixate on the problem. It's too easy to dwell on the negative and beat yourself up, forgetting about the positive, but that's not the way to fix your mixed signals. Accept and take to heart all the things your partner loves about you.

WHAT SHALL WE TALK ABOUT?

Family Meeting Discussion Openers about
Verbal Communication

Ask and answer any or all of these questions, taking turns with your partner:
1. What are your favorite things to talk about?
2. What kinds of things are difficult for you to talk about?
3. If you two need to have a difficult conversation, what might make it less stressful for you?
4. What is a loving way you two can end a difficult conversation, to remind each other that your love is more important than the issues?

Chapter 1: Verbal Mixed Signals to Fixed Signals

DATE NIGHT THEME

Verbal Communication through Alternating Topics

On this date, each of you will have a pre-determined amount of time to discuss something that you're interested in. The topic is your choice, so you can talk about whatever you like. The only rule is that when your turn is over, you stop talking about your topic, no matter how fascinating it was, so you can turn your attention to your partner's topic.

Take a short break to "clear the palate" between your turn and your partner's turn, perhaps with an appetizer or beverage, or ordering dessert if you're at a restaurant.

When you're both ready, set the timer again and let your partner choose the topic to talk about.

Most people enjoy the chance to choose what to talk about sometimes. It's nice to have someone join you in talking about your interests, and to listen to theirs, especially when that someone is the one you love.

FICTIONAL COUPLES FIXING MIXED SIGNALS

Trish & Bill

Trish and Bill moved in together after dating for a year. Their families were thrilled that they had found each other and were building a life together. It was an exciting adventure for them to find this first apartment together and make it their home. Secretly, Bill thought that he should have proposed to her before they moved in together, but that never happened. Even though he knew Trish was the one for him, the idea of the actual proposal terrified him. Somehow, the decision was made that they would live together, and he went along with it. He couldn't imagine anything better than living with Trish except being married to her.

One afternoon they were getting ready for their regular date night. They'd already picked the restaurant, one of their favorites, and they'd chosen what they would order from the menu on the website in advance. Neither of them liked the idea of trying to make any kind of decision while in a potentially stressful setting like a restaurant. At least they both enjoyed eating early, so they could miss the dinner rush.

Trish was in the bedroom putting on lipstick, and Bill was re-organizing his wallet to make sure he had everything in place, even though he knew each card in there. It calmed him to sort and re-organize things.

Chapter 1: Verbal Mixed Signals to Fixed Signals

"When do you want to leave?" Trish asked.

"Hmm ..." Bill noticed an expired credit card still in his wallet. "A couple of minutes," he said.

"Perfect." Trish checked the time, checked her hair, and got her purse. At exactly two minutes after Bill had said "a couple of minutes" she was sitting in the car ready to go.

Meanwhile, Bill realized he would have to take everything out of his wallet and double-check his cards. Was anything else expired? Where were the scissors to cut the old one up before throwing it away? How many times should he cut through it, to be really safe? He took care of business and got everything just so, then put his wallet into his pocket and looked around. He didn't see Trish. She must be in the bathroom. They both hated talking through a closed bathroom door so he would never dream of trying to hurry her. He sat down in the living room to wait.

Ten minutes later he got a text from Trish. "Are you okay?" He smiled, loving how she spelled words out in her texts rather than the shorthand, R U OK? Then he frowned. Why was she texting him from the bathroom? And why wouldn't he be okay?

"I'm fine. Ready when you are."

"I'm in the car. Where are you?"

Bill bolted to his feet and looked out the window. There she was, waving at him from the passenger seat. He whirled around and looked at the bathroom door, realizing this time that there was no light showing under the door. It had been empty the whole time, and she was waiting for him in a hot car.

He raced to the car and was out of breath by the time he got buckled in, more from his distress at making her wait than from his sprint from the house to the car.

"Why did you just come out here without telling me? I've been waiting for you in the house."

Trish looked surprised. "But, you said you'd be ready in a couple of minutes, so after two minutes I went to the car. I thought you were right behind me. What took you so long?"

"I didn't see you come out. I guess I was focused on my wallet. There was an expired card."

"Of course." Trish knew how important it was to Bill to have his wallet organized just so. "But why did you tell me you could leave in two minutes instead of saying something more accurate, like that you could leave when you finished with your wallet?"

"When I said a couple of minutes, I didn't literally mean two minutes exactly."

"But a couple is two. Like you and me." They both smiled at each other, still blissfully astonished to be a couple.

"True, but I didn't mean it literally, as in, 120 seconds. I meant a few minutes."

"How many is a few?"

"Several?"

Chapter 1: Verbal Mixed Signals to Fixed Signals

"Those are not numbers, Bill. Not helpful."

"I'm sorry, sweetheart. I forgot how much you don't like vague communication. I'll try to be clear next time."

"Thank you. And I'll try to remember to double-check with you if you say 'a couple of minutes' while you're focused on organizing something. I should have recognized that as a potential red flag."

Bill smiled sheepishly. "Thank you for not getting upset with me for being so...you know, so me."

"I love you being so you!" Trish smiled back at him. "You being you is one of my favorite things. Now, let's go. I'm starving!"

For Bill, it was important to remember that Trish takes language literally. For Trish, realizing that Bill might not be fully listening while he's organizing something was good to know.

Justin & Maggie

Maggie brought the lasagna to the table, served them each, and then watched closely while Justin took a bite.

"What do you think?" she asked expectantly.

"I think it's lasagna. What am I supposed to think?"

"I mean, do you like it?"

"I always like lasagna," said Justin. "The one we had last week was better, but this one's okay."

"Are you kidding me?" Maggie put down her fork forcefully and glowered.

Relating While Autistic

"Why would I kid about lasagna?"

"Last week we had a frozen lasagna. Today I spent five hours making this from scratch."

"Good try! Yours is almost as good as the professional one!"

Maggie burst into tears and ran to their bedroom, slamming the door behind her. Justin continued eating his lasagna, troubled by Maggie's unusual behavior but clueless as to the cause of her distress.

After several frosty days of not talking to each other more than absolutely necessary, the day came for their scheduled Family Meeting. They met at the kitchen table at their usual time and sat without speaking. Finally Justin cleared his throat.

"I don't know what's supposed to happen now," he said.

"I would have thought it would be obvious. I'm waiting for you to apologize."

"I'm sorry. I am so sorry, Maggie. So very, very sorry."

"You don't know what you're apologizing for, do you?"

"Not a clue. But I'm sure it was my fault, whatever it was."

"Do you remember when I made you a homemade lasagna from scratch, because I know it's your favorite dish?"

"Yes. That was pretty good. Is that what I'm apologizing for?"

"Justin, I spent hours and hours making that. I made the sauce from tomatoes. From actual tomatoes! And I bought that fancy rainbow pasta in the expensive section of the grocery store. And

Chapter 1: Verbal Mixed Signals to Fixed Signals

after all that work, you said you liked the frozen lasagna more than mine!"

"Well, yeah. I've been eating the same brand of frozen lasagna my whole life. I love it. You made it different, and different is not good for me. I am sorry, but I can't lie to you. I like my familiar lasagna, not your fancy weird las—"

"Weird?!?"

"Wait, rewind, I need a do-over!" Justin put his forehead down on the table and just breathed for a while. Maggie realized he was not ready to talk yet, so she just waited.

Eventually he sat back up. "I always want to say the thing that makes you smile, not the thing that makes you cry. But sometimes I don't know what the thing is. I try, but I get it wrong. Really wrong. And then I worry that this is the time you'll leave and never come back. I don't know what I'd do if you left me, but I don't know why you stay with me, either."

"Oh, Justin." Maggie reached out and took his hand. "I am not leaving you. This is just an argument. Couples have arguments all the time, but it doesn't mean they're breaking up. They talk it out. They apologize, they forgive each other, and they're okay again."

"Talking it out is not my strength," Justin said. "I never say the right thing. It helps me when you're really clear about what you want. Just tell me what you want me to say."

"That seems bossy."

"I like it when you're bossy. When I know what you want, maybe I can avoid making so many mistakes."

"Do you think this is the autism?"

"Probably. Don't you?"

"Well, what can I do that would help?"

"Keep making the same frozen lasagna. It's my favorite, I'm used to it, and I'm not good with change."

"Okay, I'll remember that."

"If I say the wrong thing, can you tell me what it was, so I can try not to keep making the same mistakes? I never want to hurt you."

"Yeah, I'll try to remember to tell you if my feelings get hurt rather than just bottling it up."

"Okay. And I'll try to think before I say something that might hurt your feelings."

For Justin and Maggie, having a regularly scheduled Family Meeting to talk about things that come up during the week was a good idea. It gave them a safe space to talk about their different communication styles, and to listen and really hear each other.

Lucia & Naima

"So, where do you want to go for dinner for our anniversary?" Naima scrolled through menus on her phone.

"Hmm…" Lucia started thinking about where she wanted to go.

Chapter 1: Verbal Mixed Signals to Fixed Signals

"Are you in the mood for Thai?"

Lucia paused in her thinking about where she wanted to go and started thinking about whether she was in the mood for Thai.

"That new place has live music on Friday nights. Would that be fun? Or maybe it'll be too crowded? Or too noisy?"

Lucia paused thinking about Thai food and started thinking about live music. Would it be fun? Would it be crowded? Would it be too noisy? And what was that first question she was supposed to answer?

"Or maybe we should try—"

"Stop! I can't stand all the constant badgering!"

"Badgering?" Naima was astonished. "I'm not badgering you."

"It's just one question after another. I can't take it anymore!"

"I only asked one question: where we should go for dinner? How is that badgering?"

"First you asked where I wanted to go. Then before I could answer you asked me if I was in the mood for Thai. Then, while I was trying to decide whether I was, you asked me, like, three questions about that new place with music. And then you were about to ask me another one! You know you were!"

Naima stood for a moment with her mouth slightly open, staring off, while she processed what Lucia said. Was that what she was doing, badgering her with a bunch of questions? It felt like she was just exploring where they should go, kind of talking it through together with her partner. But apparently that's not how it felt to Lucia.

"I'm sorry. I really had no idea that's what I was doing. I didn't mean to ask you so many questions."

Lucia nodded and took a few breaths before answering. "I can't keep track of so many questions. It jumbles up my brain."

"How can I do better? I don't mean to jumble your brain. What if I forget? I don't want to keep doing this to you."

"I appreciate that. How about if I give you a signal to let you know I'm not ready for another question? I could hold up one finger for one question at a time."

"Good idea. If I ask you a question, and then I forget and start to ask you another one, you hold up one finger and I'll stop."

"Thank you! That will be so much better!"

"Okay, now I want you to forget all the old questions I asked you before."

"What questions?"

"Exactly! I just have one question for you: Thai, yes or no?"

"Yes!"

Lucia and Naima worked out their verbal communication issue of asking multiple questions and came up with a nonverbal cue: raising an index finger to ask for only one question at a time.

And they loved the Thai restaurant.

Chapter 1: Verbal Mixed Signals to Fixed Signals

Crow & Daisy

Crow looks around the comic book store. Where's Daisy? She's usually early, and she never misses a D&D campaign. Where could she be? Crow starts wandering around the store, glancing up and down each aisle. Finally, at the back of the store, Crow sees a guy in a corner, crowding and looming over Daisy.

CROW: Hey, Daisy, it's time for D&D. You coming?

DAISY: ...

   GUY: We're talking, do you mind?

CROW: Daisy, is this a friend of yours?

DAISY: ...

   GUY: Yeah, I'm her friend, and we're trying to have a friendly conversation. Now get out of here.

CROW: (*Walks over to get a closer look, sees Daisy wide-eyed, frozen, backed into a corner*) Hey, are you okay? Do you know this guy?

DAISY: ...

   GUY: I told you, we're friends, now leave us alone!

CROW: (*Sizes up the situation and realizes Daisy needs to be rescued*) Come on, Daisy, we need you in the D&D room. Let's go.

   GUY: (*Moves to stand between Crow and Daisy, keeping her in the corner*) We're having some fun here, and we don't need you, so get out of here, you weirdo!

Relating While Autistic

DAISY: ... (*Gives her head a quick shake and starts to slide to the floor*)

CROW: I've got you, here we go. (Takes her arm, holds her up, and leads her around the guy)

GUY: I said, she's fine! Who do you think you are?

CROW: (*Ignores him, leads Daisy away. Before they get to the D&D room, Crow steers her to two chairs, and they sit*) Daisy, are you okay? Who was that guy? Was he bothering you?

DAISY: (*Takes a deep, shaky breath, and suddenly the words pour out, tumbling over each other*) I don't know him. He seemed friendly, you know? He said he wanted to be friends. He wanted to show me something in the corner, but I don't know what. He said he wanted to be good friends, and I like friends. But I don't like people pushing up so close to me. Too close! I felt weird. But, I don't know why, because his words were good, friendly words, so I don't understand why I felt so weird. I guess because I am weird. What was wrong between his words and how I felt? I couldn't figure that out, because he was saying nice things and then I froze and I couldn't move or talk.

CROW: Okay, okay, you can talk now, apparently. That guy was creeping on you.

DAISY: He was a creep? He said he wanted to be friends.

CROW: Creeps like that are dangerous, not friends. Why didn't you say something if you were uncomfortable?

Chapter 1: Verbal Mixed Signals to Fixed Signals

DAISY: Sometimes, when I'm really stressed, I just freeze. I can't talk. I don't know why, but even if I want to say something, nothing comes out.

CROW: Hey, anytime you feel weird with any of these guys that hang around here, you come find me, okay? Trust that weird feeling, and get out of there.

DAISY: And you'll be my hero? Or maybe my heroine?

CROW: Not a hero or a heroine, just a friend.

DAISY: Ha! We're friends! You just admitted it, I heard you!

CROW: I guess weirdos have to stick together.

DAISY: "When we meet in hell, we'll drink together as comrades!"

CROW: Wait, what?

DAISY: You know, from "A Nerd's Guide to D&D Battle Cries." Don't you read anything, weirdo?

CROW: Oh, I'm SOOOO glad you got your voice back. That's sarcasm, by the way.

DAISY: Convivial sarcasm? Now I know we're friends!

CROW: (*Chuckles to themself*) Weirdo.

Relating While Autistic

THEY SAY

I tend to want to say a particular word, and if I can't find it I have to put a disclaimer up like, "This isn't the word I am trying to use, but this is the closest word to my word." Then we usually have a conversation about the word I am trying to use in the context I want to use it in. Sometimes the word I end up using can hurt feelings, when that's not what I intended at all.

— Thomas McDonald III

Sometimes I forget that my wife doesn't have all the same information that I do. We're so close, I assume we're always on the same page. One day I was supposed to pick up our son from school, but his best friend's mom called to ask if she could pick up both boys and go to the park, the library, and then to their house to play until supper. They've done this kind of thing before and it's always been fine with my wife, so I said sure. When my wife got home from work and asked where our son was, I said I had no idea. I was surprised at how strongly and emotionally she reacted. When she asked if I had gone to pick him up at school, I said no again. She was extremely upset and insisted that I get in the car right that minute and go out looking for him. I said I would be happy to go out if she wanted me to, but that I assumed he was either at the park, the library, or the friend's house. Of course,

Chapter 1: Verbal Mixed Signals to Fixed Signals

she had no idea that I had made that arrangement, and I realized afterward that there was no way for her to know from the limited information I shared with her. I mean, I answered the questions she asked, but I didn't think about the questions she didn't know to ask. It's embarrassing to know you're smart, and then to have a conversation like this and feel so stupid. After that, she tried to ask me more specific questions, and I tried to imagine what she might need to know, whether she asked the right questions or not.

— Martin, ND, married to Connie, NT

One thing we do to help with communication is using participation energy percentages. We use those to determine if we are both comfortable with the energy needed for an activity. If we want to have a conversation or engage in an activity, the "Initiator" shares how much participation from the other is needed for the activity, and the "Participator" shares how much energy they have for participating. A serious conversation might need at least 80% participation to be successful. So if one of us only has 10% of participation energy, we pause the discussion until later. But just listening while one of us goes on a excited ramble about a special interest—that might only require 10% listening participation. It helped us avoid hurting each other's feelings. It's about our aligned energy levels, not disinterest in the other's ideas.

— Jordyn

Relating While Autistic

I can often get frustrated with myself when I'm trying to communicate, and then I get standoffish and short with my husband because I'm trying to sort through the layers of emotions hitting me all at once. So when that happens, I'll say, "I'm frustrated with myself," and then just say whatever is in my mind, whether it makes sense or not. Then my husband knows I'm in a state of overwhelm and helps me pause from whatever I'm doing so I can regulate. This has helped these instances not escalate into disagreements with hurt feelings, because we both understand there's more going on than what's coming out on the surface. He realizes it's not about him at all; it's about me not being kind to myself.

— Tara, autistic woman, married to a man with ADHD

With verbal communication, generally speaking, I just tell him, "I am having problems coming up with the words right now. Can you please give me some time to think about what I want to say?" That time could be five minutes, but it can also be three days. He is very patient, never in a hurry. During the interim, we are kind to each other. This is not a race, and we will not stop loving each other.

— Wendy B.

Chapter 2

Nonverbal Mixed Signals to Fixed Signals

"Nonverbal communication is an elaborate secret code that is written nowhere, known by none, and understood by all."

— Edward Sapir, anthropologist-linguist

Chapter 2: Nonverbal Mixed Signals to Fixed Signals

Nonverbal communication is a vast collection of many overt or subtle behaviors. While it is certainly true that nonverbal communication is "an elaborate secret code," as Edward Sapir wrote in the quote above, his assumption that it is "understood by all" makes me suspect he must have been neurotypical. Nonverbal communication is something that many ND people struggle with. They may choose their words carefully to say exactly what they mean and still find themselves misunderstood by their NT partners who read more into facial expression and body language than was ever intended.

There are several different kinds of nonverbal communication that people use daily, often while completely unaware of them. These include:

- *Facial Expression* — Most of us know a smile usually means the person is happy and a frown with lowered eyebrows signifies anger. Beyond the obvious ones, subtle micro-expressions can give hints about how someone really feels, whether or not the expresser or the observer is aware of what is being communicated. Or, facial expression can be completely misleading, if a person naturally lowers their eyebrows when they're concentrating or smiles when they're under stress.

Relating While Autistic

- *Eye Gaze* — NTs put a lot of stock in whether or not someone makes eye contact to decide if they are trustworthy. If you avoid eye contact, you must be lying, or so some people assume. The problem with this assumption is that many NDs are extremely uncomfortable looking right at someone's eyes. If your partner has what you consider a "shifty gaze," remember this does not mean they're lying to you. Some of the most honest people you'll ever know are on the autism spectrum, and your partner may be among them. Look beyond the presence or absence of eye contact to see the person behind the eyes.

- *Gestures* — These are movements, usually of the hands, arms, shoulders, or head. Typical gestures include nodding or shaking one's head for *yes* and *no*, waving, pointing, and holding up fingers to show how many. There are other gestures which are less easy to interpret. For example, shrugging or raising the shoulders can mean different things. If you ask someone a question and they raise both shoulders equally while holding their palms up, it often means they do not know the answer to the question. It can also mean, "Oh, well, what are you going to do?" or "Don't ask me." However, a single shoulder raised while tilting the head or turning the face in the direction of the raised shoulder may be an expression of boredom, sarcasm, or contempt, or of being dismissive of an idea that has been shared. The accompanying facial expression or gesture, such as eye-rolling, and context are important clues to understand the meaning of a shrug. If you're not sure what your partner is communicating with their gestures, ask.

- *Body Language* — You may not be aware that the way you hold your body communicates something to the people around you, but it does. An open body stance, shoulders down, back straight, arms and legs uncrossed and head up means to an NT that the person is approachable, open to discussion, and probably friendly. If your shoulders are raised up toward your ears, your back curved forward in a slouch, arms and/or legs crossed, and head facing down so that the top of your head is what they see, people may assume you are unapproachable, negative, closed to communication, and probably unfriendly. The message you're sending nonverbally through your body language or posture may or may not be what you meant to put out there, but being aware of how your partner may perceive you nonverbally can help you communicate more effectively. If you have a partner who feels safest when their body is curved protectively inward, head down, shoulders up, don't assume they mean anything negative by this posture. We don't all speak the same body language.

- *Presentation* — How you present yourself may not seem like communication, but people do pick up messages about you based on what they see, which is certainly nonverbal. If your hair is greasy and messy, or if it is clean and combed, people will have an opinion of you at first sight before you've said a word. You might love wearing the exact same outfit every day, maybe your favorite sports hero's number jersey, or purple camouflage, or an anime T-shirt. But, even if you've washed it every night or you have seven identical shirts, people will think you're wearing the same clothes and they might judge you. Consider having different versions of your favorite outfit rather than exact replicas to nonverbally communicate that yes, you are a fan, but you're a fan who wears clean clothes every day. Does appearing clean mean you are a better person? No, of course not. But, will people be more likely to avoid you if you look dirty? Perhaps. Will your partner keep you at arm's length? Maybe, but I hope not. It's not fair, but it is human nature to be more attracted to clean and tidy than to dirty and messy. Make your own choices, but make educated choices, knowing the nonverbal message that people may read into your physical presentation.

Chapter 2: Nonverbal Mixed Signals to Fixed Signals

- *Touch* — Many NTs, especially women, communicate feelings by touch: a hand on an arm, an arm around a shoulder, a sympathetic hug. However, many NDs are oversensitive and may avoid touch. Make sure you and your partner are on the same page when it comes to communicating through touch.

- *Paralinguistics* — It's not what you say, it's how you say it. Paralinguistics includes tone, volume, pitch, and other nuances. Some people with attention-deficit/hyperactivity disorder (ADHD) may talk quickly. Some, but not all, autistic people may use a pedantic, formal tone of voice. People who speak in an unusually high-pitched voice may seem childish, and those who raise their voices at the end of every sentence, like a question, may sound uncertain. When you're communicating with your partner, remember to pay attention not only to the content, but also the nonverbal tone of the message. However, don't be misled by paralinguistics. Don't treat someone with a high voice as if they were a child, and don't assume that a person who naturally raises their voice in a questioning tone doesn't know what they're talking about. Listen to their words, and believe them.

Relating While Autistic

- *Text* — Punctuation, capitalization, and emojis are also forms of nonverbal communication and may be misunderstood. Many younger people view a period at the end of a text as icy or rude, whereas boomers habitually end every sentence with punctuation, whether it's in a handwritten letter or a quick text message. Some people use /s to signify that a statement was sarcastic, and others use emojis to convey their emotional state without writing a single word.

What are nonverbal danger points—mixed signals that trip up so many couples? Let's explore a few of these Red Lights below, with Green Light solutions offered to fix those mixed signals.

RED LIGHT/GREEN LIGHT TIPS FOR NONVERBAL COMMUNICATION

 RED LIGHT: Intentions Misunderstood

 Green Lights:

- Do tell your partner you welcome their feedback if something you communicate misses the mark. If they are using nonverbal cues to add unintended meaning to the words you chose, you can set them straight.

Chapter 2: Nonverbal Mixed Signals to Fixed Signals

- Do be mindful if your partner is someone who doesn't usually show a wide range of expressions on their face, rather than making assumptions based on nonverbal signals. If you're not sure what they intended to communicate, ask them what they meant. Then believe them.

 RED LIGHT: Facial Expression Doesn't Match Words

 Green Lights:

- Do put more emphasis on the words spoken than on the nonverbal communication. Your partner may have chosen their words carefully and mean exactly what they say.
- Do check in to make sure you understand the intended message if their words and facial expressions don't seem to match.

Relating While Autistic

DATE NIGHT THEME

You Don't Say

Just for fun, agree to a set amount of time on your date to communicate only nonverbally. Point, wave, shrug, use exaggerated facial expressions, anything but spoken words. See how well you can get your feelings and ideas across to one another without using speech. If it becomes uncomfortable for either of you, then stop. This is intended to be fun, not stressful.

WHAT SHALL WE TALK ABOUT?

Family Meeting about Nonverbal Communication

What's your favorite thing to do when you have a free day all to yourself?

Imagine you're doing it. Consider miming or acting it out if you're comfortable doing so. How do you feel when you engage in this activity? How does your face look? Take turns sharing your favorite thing and feelings about it.

If it would be fun for both of you, consider playing "How Do I Feel?" by showing a facial expression that you use when

Chapter 2: Nonverbal Mixed Signals to Fixed Signals

you feel a certain emotion, and see if your partner can guess it. There are no wrong answers here. Some people smile when they are under extreme stress and may appear sad or angry when they feel perfectly happy. This is a good opportunity to learn more about how your loved one expresses their emotions without saying a word.

FICTIONAL COUPLES FIXING MIXED SIGNALS

Trish & Bill

Bill checked his pocket for the fiftieth time. Yes, the small box was still there. He bit the inside of his cheek and tried to steady his ragged breathing. If he could stay calm and get through this evening, his world would be forever changed.

But, changed in what way? Does she love him or love him not? Was true happiness to be or not to be? Would it be the best of times or the worst of times? Would the course of true love never run smooth? And would he be able to stop thinking in quotes and cliches long enough to just ask her already?

When Trish got home from work, he surprised her with her favorite casserole already in the oven. He had thought about flowers and candles too late to actually get them, but he hoped the table looked nice anyway.

Relating While Autistic

"What a nice surprise!" she said. "What's the occasion?"

That stopped him. How to answer? If he told her the occasion was that he was about to propose to her, that would spoil it. How could he sidestep her question and get on the right track?

"Trish, we need to talk." There was a long pause.

"No," she whispered. "Please don't."

Now he was terrified. She didn't want him to propose. In fact, she looked devastated. Her face lost its color, and her eyes were filling up with tears. Not happy tears, either; he could see that. She didn't want to marry him. But he already had the ring in his pocket. He felt like a train on a track. He had to keep going, even if he saw that the bridge was out. He fumbled the box out of his pocket and dropped to one knee. Trish slumped to the floor and sat beside him with her face in her hands.

"Trish, I have to ask you something important."

"Please don't! I don't want to break up!" Now she was crying.

Bill opened the box and held the ring in front of her face, but her eyes were tightly shut with tears squeezing out of the corners and dripping off her chin.

"I don't want to break up either," he said. He waved the ring back and forth in front of her face, but she didn't look.

"Then why are you doing this?" she sobbed.

"Because I love you and I want to spend the rest of my life with you."

Chapter 2: Nonverbal Mixed Signals to Fixed Signals

"If that were true, you wouldn't be breaking up with me!"

"I'm not! I'm proposing! Trish, will you marry me?" There, he got it out. In a moment, when she said no, his world would start imploding, but at least he had said what he had to say first. It was done.

"What?" Trish hiccupped once and then stopped sobbing. She blinked.

"I'm asking you to marry me."

"Marry you?"

"I wish you'd answer me. I can't bear this. Will you marry me?" He held the ring out again and she saw it for the first time.

"But you looked so angry, and you said, 'We need to talk.' That's what people say when they're about to break up."

"I didn't know that. I thought it was what they said when they wanted to talk. And I'm not angry, I'm terrified. You still haven't said yes or no."

Trish threw her arms around him and started crying again. "Yes, yes, yes, of course I'll marry you!" Bill could tell that these were happy tears. He hugged her back, relief spreading through him like, like a wave, like a wave of...like some cliche that he couldn't think of right now because he was far too busy hugging his fiancée.

Relating While Autistic

Justin & Maggie

Maggie came in wearing a new dress. "What do you think?" she asked, giving a twirl.

"It looks very nice," Justin said. She stood still and looked at him, her smile fading.

"You don't like it."

"Of course I like it, I said it looks very nice."

"No, you're just saying that to spare my feelings. I can see how you really feel. It's written all over your face."

"I don't believe that's accurate," said Justin. "I said it looked nice because it does look nice. I wouldn't lie to you."

"It's obvious you don't really like it."

"Please explain to me in what way that is obvious, since in fact I do like it."

"Come here," she said, and led him by the hand to a mirror. "Now, look in the mirror, and tell me how you like my new dress."

"I like your new dress. It looks very nice. What part of that do you not understand? It seems entirely unambiguous."

"But look at your face," she insisted. "You're not smiling, you look grumpy, there's not a hint of enjoyment or pleasure."

"That's just my face. It's always like that."

"When we were in plays together, you were expressive."

"Acting!" Justin emoted with a flourish.

"So, it was all pretend?"

Chapter 2: Nonverbal Mixed Signals to Fixed Signals

"Absolutely. In real life I have a resting blank face."

"Okay. Oh, by the way, someone at the office was asking for a recommendation of a good video game to try. I thought about suggesting the crafting game you always play, but I didn't know what to tell them. I mean, what's so great about that game?"

"Are you kidding me? Crafting games offer rich, visually stimulating virtual environments that are highly imaginative, but with a well-designed structure. They provide clear visual clues, well-defined expectations, positive reinforcement, and—why are you laughing?"

"Look at yourself." Maggie turned Justin toward the mirror, and he caught a glimpse of his animated, excited, smiling expression before it settled back into his usual deadpan. "I wish your face would light up when you look at me the way it does when you talk about video games."

He smiled. "Well, you do offer visual stimulation and positive reinforcement, and I have to say you have a well-designed structure, but where are the clear cues and well-defined expectations? That's what I need."

"I really want to know, Justin. Why don't you smile at me that way? I hope you don't love video games more than you love me."

"Do you really think that?" Justin was appalled, until she laughed.

Relating While Autistic

"Not really, I was kidding. Mostly. I know you love me, but you seem so much more excited when you're talking about your game."

"I don't plan how my face is going to look when I talk about games, or about you. I don't know how to make myself smile on purpose. If you want proof, my mom has thirteen years of school pictures that show me awkwardly trying to smile. I always thought I nailed it, until the pictures came back. Gruesome!"

"But smiling is easy, it's natural."

"You think that because you're neurotypical. It is easy for you, but not for me."

"So, when you look at me with a straight face and say you love me, or the dinner is delicious, or I look stunning in my new dress, I should take you at your word, not your face, and accept it as a compliment, right?"

"Exactly! Believe my words. Unless I say something that makes you mad. Then please assume I didn't mean it the way it came out. And give me do-overs when I blow it, which I probably will."

"Okay, do-overs sounds doable."

"Thank you. And you do look stunning in that dress."

For Justin and Maggie, being aware that his facial expressions might not always tell the whole story and giving do-overs in case of misunderstandings went a long way towards improving their communication.

Chapter 2: Nonverbal Mixed Signals to Fixed Signals

Lucia & Naima

Naima came home from work and started pacing in her usual pattern: around the perimeter of the living room, around the kitchen island, down the hall, and back to the living room. On her fourth pass, Lucia spoke.

"I'm guessing you had a bad day."

"You think?" Naima didn't slow down. Back around the island.

"Yeah, I can tell. Do you want to talk about it?"

"Later. I need five more rounds."

After five more cycles of pattern walking, she came and sat beside Lucia on the couch. "Something's wrong at work."

"What is it?"

"I have no idea."

"Then how do you know something's wrong?" Lucia asked. "Maybe it's just your imagination."

"My imagination is not that good."

"So, what are the clues that made you think something was wrong?"

"Well, my boss looks angry. His eyebrows are down, his eyes look down, and his mouth is down at the edges. Angry."

"Or maybe tired. Do you think he might be tired instead of angry?"

"Hmm...his wife just had a baby, actually, and he talks a lot about not getting any sleep. Do you really think he might be just tired instead of angry?"

Relating While Autistic

"Well, I'm not an expert on facial expressions. Let's Google it." They searched for images of tired faces. The first few they found were extremely exaggerated, like a huge yawn, or falling asleep on a desk. Not helpful. Finally they found some more realistic images of tired facial expressions.

"Actually, that looks more like my boss today," Naima said. "Do you think maybe he's not mad at me after all?"

"Well, I don't really know. Did you do anything to make him mad?"

"I do the same things every day. Nothing new, nothing unusual."

"So, there's nothing for him to be mad at you about. Since his face matches one of the tired images, and you know he's losing sleep with a newborn at home, I'm guessing he's not mad at you at all. He's probably just exhausted."

"Well, that's a relief. I really can't read people at all. The safest default seems to be assuming they're mad at me, but I guess that's not always the case."

"Okay, look at my face and tell me how I'm feeling." Lucia crossed her eyes and stuck out her tongue.

"You're hungry," guessed Naima.

"I am, actually! You could tell that from my facial expression?"

"No, but it's seven o'clock and we haven't had dinner yet."

Lucia laughed. "You got me."

Chapter 2: Nonverbal Mixed Signals to Fixed Signals

Naima had trouble decoding facial expressions, but talking it over with Lucia reminded her not to assume the worst when in doubt about nonverbal signals.

Crow & Daisy

Crow and Daisy are on the bus on the way to a Dungeons & Dragons convention. Daisy has been talking non-stop, full speed, at a high pitch, from the moment they arrived at the bus stop.

CROW: So, I guess you're not too excited about the Con.

DAISY: Of course I'm excited! Who wouldn't be excited? Aren't you excited?

CROW: (*Chuckling*) That was sarcasm. You've been talking faster than I thought humanly possible in a voice so high only dogs can hear it. No one could miss your excitement.

DAISY: You're excited, too. I can tell by the way you don't look at all excited, and yet, here we are on the bus to the Con. So I infer your excitement, however miserly you are with it.

CROW: Miserly? Fair enough, I guess. I mean, I'm excited, but I like to be cool. Don't want to be the most excited person in the room.

DAISY: Well, for your information, every room has to have a most excited person in it. That's science. So, why shouldn't it be you? Why let someone else have all the fun?

Relating While Autistic

CROW: Huh. That actually makes sense, in a weird way.

DAISY: Yeah, it does. So, are you embarrassed to hang around with the most excited girl on the bus?

CROW: I guess I can tolerate it.

DAISY: You are charmed and delighted. I can read it all over your completely blank face.

CROW: You can't tell that. My blank face is inscrutable, and I am as unknowable as the wind at midnight!

DAISY: Oh, I know who you are: mundane human by day, level 15 chaotic-neutral half-elf cleric by night. You are utterly charmed and delighted by the most excited chaotic-good dwarf on the bus.

CROW: Okay, I give up, I could never argue with a cute chaotic-good dwarf.

DAISY: You think I'm cute?

CROW: I didn't say—

DAISY: You think I'm cute! You do! That's okay, I think you're cute, too.

CROW: I'm not cute! I'm dark and mysterious.

DAISY: I know you think you are. That's one of the cutest things about you.

Chapter 2: Nonverbal Mixed Signals to Fixed Signals

THEY SAY

I tend to say things as they are processed in my head, and for the most part it doesn't come across the way I wanted. For example, I have a plain or staunch face while saying the food was delicious. I don't mean to have that face, and I do like the food, but that isn't always what's conveyed.

— Thomas McDonald III

When we first began living together, there were a lot of misunderstandings. I would think he was much angrier than he was, he would think I was much more serious than I was, and we would find ourselves frustrated and feeling confused. We then thought to add in scales so we could better calibrate with each other. We came up with a scale of 1 to 5 and determined what the scores meant together. When we felt confused about a perspective, we would ask the other to share how serious/upset/joking they were on a scale of 1 to 5. It helped us eliminate confusion. We used the scale a LOT. Now that we understand each other better, we don't have to use it as often, but it's still super helpful when we don't feel like we're on the same page.

— Jordyn

Relating While Autistic

When I get very upset, I tend to shut down. This is unintentional, and my partner knows I am not doing this on purpose. Sometimes I hide in the house because I am so frightened. He finds me. He speaks gently and draws me out. When I do come out, he holds me or holds my hand. He tells me he loves me and I can talk if I want, or not if I am not yet ready. This allows me to stop spinning out inside my head. I calm down and eventually feel safe enough to speak up.

— Wendy B.

Chapter 3

Social Mixed Signals to Fixed Signals

"Electric communication will never be a substitute for the face of someone who with their soul encourages another person to be brave and true."

— Charles Dickens

Chapter 3: Social Mixed Signals to Fixed Signals

S ocial communication is one of the most important things to attend to in order to have a relationship that thrives. It's also one of the hallmark challenges shared by many neurodivergent individuals. Does this mean that ND couples can't make it work? Of course not. Every couple can share their feelings with each other, respecting and honoring each partner's unique style. Remember that no matter what communication mixed messages might pop up, the two of you can sort it out and fix your messages before social communication problems escalate.

 RED LIGHT/GREEN LIGHT TIPS FOR SOCIAL COMMUNICATION

 RED LIGHT: Difficulty Communicating Emotions

 Green Lights:
- Do ask your partner how they feel, and believe their words when they tell you, whether or not their nonverbal communication matches their words.
- Do remember that you and your partner are two different people with different brains and different emotions. You can't assume they will feel the same way you feel in any given situation.

Relating While Autistic

 RED LIGHT: Increased Stress in Social Situations

 Green Lights:

- Do bear in mind that it may be more difficult for you or your partner to communicate in a highly social situation, such as at a party.
- Do be mindful of your partner's tolerance for social events, and be prepared to help them make a graceful exit if needed.
- Do come up with a secret signal that you both understand, in case either one of you needs to leave the party early.
- Do act immediately when you see the signal. Don't wait. Help your loved one escape from the potentially overwhelming social situation. They would do the same for you.

WHAT SHALL WE TALK ABOUT?

Family Meeting Discussion Openers about
Social Communication

Ask and answer any or all of these questions, taking turns with your partner:

Chapter 3: Social Mixed Signals to Fixed Signals

1. What's your favorite kind of social event?
2. What's your most hated social event?
3. If you both share the same favorite kind of social event, get out your calendars and find a time to do that together.
4. Do you have to attend a hated social event? This may be because someone you love is getting married, graduating, or meeting another important milestone. If the person is important enough for you to go out and be social, plan in advance to make the occasion more bearable. What will you wear? You should be comfortable. How will you get there? Be aware if social exhaustion leaves you unable to drive safely afterwards. Who will you see? It might help to make a list of people who'll be attending to help you remember. If you need to introduce your partner to new people, get everyone's name right. Does it help you to have a script of things to say or ask people? It can help to make a mental reminder to ask Aunt Bonnie about her new grandbaby. Plan an exit strategy. Don't forget to plan for extended recovery time afterward, with no other social obligations. You deserve to take care of yourself after a socially stressful situation.

Relating While Autistic

DATE NIGHT THEME

A Tale of Two Date Nights

If you each have a type of social event that you love but that the other doesn't love so much, consider setting two date nights and taking turns with each type of event. If one of you likes sports and one likes Renaissance Faire, you could get tickets for a game and also for the Faire, with enough time between the two dates to recover fully. The one who loves the event must be prepared to give their partner an out if necessary, such as leaving at halftime of the game or finding a shady spot at the Faire to read a book rather than seeing every single booth and performance. Take care that no one gets burned out, and don't try something that is known to be absolutely horrible for the other person, just things that are not preferred but tolerable. Trying the kind of social event your partner enjoys is a good way to show how much you care for them. Be sure to talk it out before and discuss it afterward to see how each of you felt about it. It may be something you never try again, or you may find a new favorite date night option.

Chapter 3: Social Mixed Signals to Fixed Signals

FICTIONAL COUPLES

Trish & Bill

Bill smiled as he sat at the dining room table waiting for Trish to bring cups of tea for their Family Meeting. He loved being a family with Trish. Living with her and being engaged to her was blissful, ecstatic, a dream come true. Then he looked down at the bridal magazines on the table and was filled with dread. The idea of standing up in front of a crowd of people, even their closest friends and family, was appalling. He imagined all of those eyes making invisible lines to land on him like the red dot of a sniper rifle, but without the escape of actually being shot in the head.

Bill shook his head rapidly. He had to get rid of negative thoughts. This was no time to be morbid. The news that popped up on his phone was difficult to cope with, so much violence everywhere. How could humans do such things to each other?

He shook his head again. Mustn't go down that rabbit hole and get stuck in the bad news loop. He pulled out his phone and deleted the news app. That would help. If anything really important happened in the news, the comedians they watched each night would mention it.

But, back to the problem of the wedding, and everyone staring. He wasn't sure if he could go through with it. When he proposed, he imagined spending the rest of his life with Trish as husband and wife, but he hadn't thought about being a bride and groom. What could he tell her? She would be crushed if he didn't go through with it. All women wanted a big wedding, right? Not that he knew what women wanted, but that much seemed clear. A big wedding with lots of bridesmaids and flowers and people staring was expected. For Trish, he would force himself to do it. She deserved to be happy.

Trish was bogged down in wedding planning. Actually, she hadn't started yet. She was still bogged down, thinking about getting around to intending to plan the wedding. Probably. But there were so many questions. Where to have it? When? How many people? She didn't want to disappoint Bill, but if they invited everyone in both of their families and everyone they worked with, well, the idea stressed her out. She paced in the kitchen, waiting for the water to boil for tea, dreading having to go back and face Bill. He expected her to plan the wedding, and she was failing. It was the bride's job, after all, and apparently most brides enjoyed it. Trish could hardly think about the wedding without wanting to run away as far and as fast as she could.

Of course, she would never run away from Bill. She loved him too much. So much so, in fact, that she would even put up with this whole wedding thing, since he wanted to get married. She was thrilled that he proposed. The deep, warm feeling of security,

Chapter 3: Social Mixed Signals to Fixed Signals

knowing that they would spend the rest of their lives together, was beyond anything she had hoped for. All she had to do was to plan the perfect wedding to make him proud. And that's where she was utterly floundering.

When the kettle whistled, she made the tea and brought it to the dining room, where Bill waited. She sat and looked down at the happy, smiling brides on the magazine covers. They made it look so easy. She felt useless.

"So," she began shakily, "about this whole wedding planning."

"Yes." Bill pasted on a smile he hoped looked sincere. "Yes, the wedding planning. Great fun. Great."

"I guess the usual thing is to find a venue, like a church or a hotel or a garden."

"Hm. Yes. Those all sound fine."

"And then who to invite. How many people."

"People. I guess that's to be expected."

"That's what I understand." Trish slid a magazine towards herself but didn't open it. "Apparently couples often have a service in one place, like a church or garden, and then have a big reception somewhere else, like a hotel, with music and dancing and all that."

"I guess that's what we should do then." Bill worked a bit harder to keep his smile in place.

"What would that be like for you?" she asked.

Relating While Autistic

"A nightmare." The truth came out automatically. He couldn't lie to Trish, but it sounded terrible. The whole idea felt terrible, so he guessed that was about right, but this was no way to talk to his bride-to-be about her special day. "By nightmare, of course, I mean, uh ... a dream?"

"Bill, if a wedding would be a nightmare for you, then we can't do it. It's your day, too, not just mine. I won't have you put up with a nightmare on my account."

"You know I would go through it for you, Trish. I love you. You deserve to have your wedding day exactly as you want it. Don't worry about me, I can put up with anything for one day if it means spending my life with you."

"But it's not what I want."

Bill froze. Did she not want to marry him? Had she changed her mind? This was bad. "It's not what you want? You don't want to marry me?"

"Of course I want to marry you! I mean, I want to be married to you for the rest of my life. I just don't want to plan a wedding. It's not fun, and it's stressing me out."

"So, let me understand this. You do want to marry me, you just don't want a wedding, is that it?"

"Yes, exactly!"

Bill grinned, a natural, happy grin, and felt his shoulders relax. "This is no problem."

Chapter 3: Social Mixed Signals to Fixed Signals

"It feels like a problem." Trish looked pointedly at the pile of bridal magazines.

In one wave of his arm Bill swept the magazines off onto the floor. "You have nothing to worry about. Leave everything to me."

"What do you mean?"

He got down on one knee. "Trish, will you marry me in a courthouse with no guests, no flowers, no music, and no hoopla?"

Trish giggled. "No hoopla?"

"No hoop, no la, no worries."

"Yes!" She threw her arms around his neck. "Yes, Bill, I will marry you anywhere, the less hoopla the better!"

"Thank goodness!" Bill breathed a sigh of relief. "I don't want you to worry about a thing, I'll take care of all the arrangements. And there's one more thing I want you to know that I will take care of."

"What's that?"

"I'll pick up all those magazines off the floor."

Relating While Autistic

Justin & Maggie

"Do we have to go?" Justin adjusted his tie again, and it still felt like it was strangling him.

"She's your only sister, and she's getting married. Yes, we have to go. Let me help you with that." Maggie straightened his tie, and Justin waited until she turned away to put in her earrings before discreetly loosening it again.

"I hate crowds. My aunt will hug me and I'll smell like her horrible perfume all day. Do you really want me to smell like my aunt?"

"You're washable."

Justin sighed. "I just don't know if I can take it. I'm afraid I'll have a meltdown and ruin everything, like I usually do."

Maggie turned to him, took his hands, and they sat together.

"What parts of the wedding do you think will be the worst?"

He rapidly ticked off on his fingers, "Crowds, smells, music, chit-chat, listening to everyone eat, smelling like my aunt, the DJ, fluorescent lights, photographers, and this tie. I'm out of fingers, but I'm sure I'll think of more things when we get there."

"That is a lot." Maggie put her arm around him. "Let me see how much of that we can take care of. You'll have to be there for the actual ceremony, and they'll want at least one photo with the bride's family. Try to stand at the back. The reception is another thing."

Chapter 3: Social Mixed Signals to Fixed Signals

"The worst."

"Hey, how do you feel about the kids? Want to hang out with your nieces and nephews?"

"Of course, I'm their fun uncle. The funcle."

"Perfect. I volunteered to help watch the kids, but I'll trade you. I'll socialize with your family, and you can spend most of the time being the funcle with the kids. Don't worry, you won't be the only one on kid duty, so you can step out if you need to take a break."

"Okay, so if I stick it out through the ceremony and the family photo, I can escape and hang with the kids? That would be great. But what if I still get overwhelmed? There's so much noise and sensory stuff. Can we leave early if I need to?"

"Of course, once the ceremony is over, we can bail whenever you need to. Just text me."

"What should I text?"

"How about, the crazy-face emoji? Then I'll know that the kids are driving you crazy and I'll come rescue you. One of the other aunts or funcles can take over."

"That's the emoji with the different-sized eyes, and tongue sticking out?"

"That's the one. You know, I think I'll check in on you a few times by text during the reception. I'll send you a question mark, and you send me a thumbs-up if you're still okay. If I don't get a thumbs-up back from you, I will come and find you."

Relating While Autistic

"Okay. This is starting to sound not completely horrible."

"Yeah, that's your sister's wedding theme, 'Not Completely Horrible.'" They laughed, hugged, and went to the wedding.

Justin could relax a bit, knowing that Maggie would swoop in and rescue him before he got overloaded and had a sensory or social meltdown. Knowing she understood and had his back made it possible for him to be there for his sister's wedding.

Lucia & Naima

"Did you see that the Official *Supernatural* Convention is coming to our state?" Lucia held up her phone so Naima could see the screen. "We should go!"

"How far away is it?"

"Only a couple of hours. I thought you'd be excited! Don't you want to meet Misha?"

"Of course. You know how I feel about Misha. But it's not like we would actually meet any of the guys. They'll be on stage, and we'll be in the crowds looking at them on the Jumbotron." Naima turned back to her book. "We might as well watch them on TV."

"We do that all the time." Lucia slumped a bit, looking at her phone. "It would be worth the crowds and the noise and the drive to be there in person."

"For you, but not so much for me. I can't ignore all that sensory chaos."

Chapter 3: Social Mixed Signals to Fixed Signals

"We haven't gone out and done anything in a long time. I just thought this would be fun."

Naima put down her book. "I'm sorry, Lucia. I do want to go out and do things with you. I love you. But that would be hard for me, that's all I'm saying."

"What would be fun for you?"

Naima thought, then she brightened up. "I know, the State Garden! It's right here in town, we wouldn't have to drive far, and there wouldn't be too many people if we go during the week. I'd love to see it!"

"That doesn't sound like much fun to me. I mean, I love trees and flowers, and walking hand in hand with you through a garden would be heaven, but I can already feel my allergies acting up just thinking about it."

"So what are we supposed to do? Have completely separate lives? That's not why I married you." Naima scooted over until they were shoulder to shoulder on the couch. "I want to spend time with my sweetheart."

"I want that, too." Lucia took her hand. "But we like such different things."

"Actually, we like a lot of the same things, we just enjoy them in different ways. We both like gardens, but your allergies drive you crazy. We both like *Supernatural*, but the crowds at a convention are too much for me."

Relating While Autistic

"I see where you're going with this." Lucia turned to face Naima without letting go of her hand. "We should find a way to do both things together, with a plan to make it more tolerable."

"Of course!" Naima smiled. "I could wear my headphones to the Con and make an escape plan if it all gets to be too much."

"That would be great!" Lucia grinned back at her. "And if I wear my strongest mask to the garden and take antihistamines before we go, maybe my allergies won't keep me from enjoying nature with you."

"A garden with my flower!" Naima said. "That's my idea of a dream date!"

"And mine is to spend time with my angel...Misha!" They both laughed. "I'll buy us tickets for one-on-one autograph and photo sessions with Misha," Lucia offered. "During the big panel discussions, you could go hang out in a coffee shop if you need to. We'll keep in touch by text, and we can always leave early if you need to."

"Lucia, thank you! I can't wait!" Naima did jazz hands in excitement, thinking about meeting Misha Collins in person. "And at the garden, if your allergies bother you, we can duck into the restaurant and enjoy the garden through the window over brunch."

"You know I love brunch!"

For Lucia and Naima, taking turns doing their favorite things, planning accommodations to reduce the impact of social, sensory,

Chapter 3: Social Mixed Signals to Fixed Signals

and allergy stressors, meant they could each enjoy their preferred social activity with their beloved.

Crow & Daisy

Daisy and Crow are waiting at the bus stop together after D&D.

DAISY: So, I guess we're a couple now.

CROW: We're not a couple. Who says we're a couple?

DAISY: Everybody knows we're a couple. In D&D, they always refer to us as "Daisy & Crow," never separately.

CROW: That doesn't mean anything. And I think they say, "Crow & Daisy." But it still doesn't mean we're a couple.

DAISY: Maybe not, but holding hands means we're a couple.

(*Crow looks down at their hands, surprised to see them intertwined. How long had they been holding hands?*)

CROW: How long have we been holding hands?

DAISY: If you mean how long have we been holding hands today, about twenty minutes. If you mean how long since the first time we held hands, two weeks and one day.

CROW: Huh. (*Crow continues looking at their hands, somewhat surprised but without letting go, then shrugs and looks away.*) Doesn't mean we're a couple. I just have to hold your hand so you don't get lost on your way home.

DAISY: (Laughing) I'm a grown-ass woman. I've been riding buses since before you were old enough to do your own laundry. (Looks closely at Crow's T-shirt) You do your own laundry, don't you?"

CROW: You and your personal questions. (*Tries unsuccessfully to hide a small smile*)

DAISY: All I'm saying is, we spend a lot of time together, not just in D&D. We text every morning. We talk on the phone every night. We hold hands. And we like each other. We are a couple. I rest my case.

CROW: Okay, I will admit that you are the least objectionable human I know—

DAISY: You sweet-talker! I like you, too.

CROW: I wasn't finished. Okay, I do like you, but that doesn't mean we're a couple. I can't be a couple with you, or with anyone.

DAISY: What do you mean, you can't? You're doing it, right now.

CROW: I can't be a couple with anyone because I'm Ace.

DAISY: You're aces in my book.

CROW: I'm not aces, I'm Ace. Asexual. As in, I don't want to have sex with you or anyone. That's what Ace means.

DAISY: Did I ask you to have sex with me?

CROW: Well, you're talking about us being a couple. I assumed.

DAISY: Assumed? Well, you know what that makes you—

CROW: Please, don't. I'm not in the mood.

Chapter 3: Social Mixed Signals to Fixed Signals

DAISY: I guess if you're asexual, you're never "in the mood," but don't make assumptions about me. Maybe I'm asexual, too, did you ever think about that?

CROW: No, I never thought about it before, but now that I am thinking about it, you're definitely not.

DAISY: Well, now I know you're a man, because that was one of the most patronizing, mansplaining things you've ever said to me.

CROW: I'm sorry, Daisy—

DAISY: Wait, I take it back. If you're apologizing, you can't be a man.

CROW: Well, that's a pretty simplistic view of the genders. You know I'm not a man or a woman, and I'll thank you not to label me.

DAISY: Yeah, I know, you're nonbinary. You're my NB, and I'm your ND. Hey, we'd be indistinguishable to someone with dyslexia! Did you know that?

CROW: I seldom know what you're talking about.

DAISY: You know, nb, nd, dyslexia, letter reversals. You get it, right?

CROW: (*Chuckling*) It is never a dull moment with you.

DAISY: I know. That's why we're such a cute couple.

CROW: You know that's not going to happen. I told you, I'm asexual.

Relating While Autistic

DAISY: And I also know that you know me. You know who I am, Crow, and not very many people can say that. Do you honestly believe that what you have, or don't have, in your pants is what's important to me? Do you think sex is all there is to being a couple?

CROW: People seem to place a lot of value on it.

DAISY: You watch too many rom-coms. There's more to being a couple than just sex. I can't believe I have to tell you that.

CROW: Here's the bus. I guess we have a lot more to talk about, but it will have to wait. I am not having this conversation on public transportation.

DAISY: That's okay. We have plenty of time. In fact, we have our whole future together—(*Smiles at Crow*)—as a couple.

THEY SAY

We communicate very well together socially. It's other people outside my relationship I get mixed signals from. My partner is very good at picking up what I mean versus what comes out of my mouth. I am very well-intentioned, but often I come across totally wrong. He has often saved me from embarrassment, and if I am embarrassing he never shames me for it. He understands I am trying. He helps me find my way to express myself better.

— Wendy B.

PART II

LOOK! For Unique Love Languages

(Sort it Out)

Gary Chapman wrote *The 5 Love Languages* and other books on the topic to help couples get on the same page when it comes to communicating their love. Learn more about his work at https://5LoveLanguages.com.

Amythest Schaber took these love languages a step further and created the *5 Neurodivergent Love Languages*. You can read more about it at https://stimpunks.org.

We'll be talking about both of their takes on love languages, and what neurodivergent couples can learn from them, in the next five chapters.

Chapter 4

Loving Words

"Better than a thousand hollow words is one word that brings peace."

— Buddha

Chapter 4: Loving Words

One of the five love languages Gary Chapman describes in his book *The 5 Love Languages* is what he calls Words of Affirmation. He writes that this love language uses words, whether spoken or written, to affirm other people.

All love languages are two-way streets, illustrating the give and take of a relationship, and the language of loving words is no different. There is the expressive side, the desire to give your partner words of love, as well as the receptive side, the desire to hear or read words of love from your partner. Those who resonate with loving words may relate to the expressive side, the receptive side, or both.

People with expressive loving words as a strength love to use words to show their partner how much they care. Sending an affectionate text, speaking words of encouragement or adoration, and finding the perfect sentiment to write on an anniversary card are all ways that they demonstrate their love. Those who do not have this language hard-wired into them may become tongue-tied when trying to express their love. They may struggle to find the right words and never feel they get it right. This doesn't mean they love less, only that expressive loving words is not their strongest way of communicating their love.

Hearing or reading loving words is important to those who have the receptive love language of loving words. This person might crave an extra "I love you" before their partner goes off to work, a haiku or heart on the bathroom mirror, or long, poetic love letters. Whatever the form, these expressions touch the heart of the person whose receptive love language is loving words. They glow when hearing, reading, or remembering the loving words of their partner and feel uplifted and appreciated by words. For them, receiving words of love is vital to feeling loved.

Not everyone shares this feeling. Some people feel uncomfortable or embarrassed hearing themselves praised, especially publicly. If one partner keeps heaping on effusive words of love while the other partner cringes, they are on different wavelengths.

Knowing your own and your partner's love languages is an important first step in improving your communication and deepening your relationship. You can find out how your partner feels about words of love by talking it over at a family meeting, or even on a date night, as long as it's not a touchy or stressful subject for either of you. You could also take Gary Chapman's quiz at https://5LoveLanguages.com/quizzes and discuss your results together.

Not all neurodivergent people are the same, any more than all neurotypical people are the same, and one size does not fit all. If Chapman's love languages don't speak to you, you might relate to Amythest Schraber's 5 *ND Love Language*, which explores Infodumping.

Chapter 4: Loving Words

One meaning of Infodumping is sharing information about a topic that you care about with a person that you care about. When you really love something, it means a lot to share it with your partner. The characterization of such sharing as "dumping" refers to the fact that there is often a great deal of information to share, and the words may pour out rapidly if the speaker is excited about the topic. In the context of a loving relationship, infodumping can be a sign of trust and a desire for closeness. This is one example of a social initiation, reaching out, or what relationship expert John Gottman calls an emotional bid.

RED LIGHT/GREEN LIGHT TIPS FOR LOVING WORDS

 RED LIGHT: Difficulty Expressing Love Using Words

 Green Lights:

- Do let your partner know that you love them, even if you don't easily put your love into words.
- Do ask your partner what kinds of loving expressions they most appreciate. You may be surprised to learn that they'd rather see you wink at them across the room than write them a sonnet. Remember, winking, smiling, throwing a kiss, or making "heart hands" all

express loving words which are understood, even if they are nonverbal.

- Do find a way to communicate your love, even if words are not your strength. You can't opt out of expressing your love in ways that your partner needs. Being in love means going out of your way for your beloved, so avoid becoming complacent in your relationship.
- Do find new ways to help you express your love, especially if you know that loving words are important to your partner. This might mean making a note to yourself or a calendar reminder to compliment or express your love to your partner at least three times a day. Make a list of all the things you love about them, and refer to the list for inspiration. This doesn't mean you have to become a Shakespeare-quoting poet; words of love in written form, even very brief ones, mean a lot. You might use sticky notes, emojis, refrigerator word magnets, texts, or brief emails to declare your love. It's important to send a message, even if it's just a heart-eyes emoji, so that your beloved knows that you're thinking loving thoughts of them.

Chapter 4: Loving Words

 RED LIGHT: **Difficulty Receiving Love Using Words**

 Green Lights:

- Do tell your partner how you feel about when, where, or how you enjoy receiving loving words. If you cringe inwardly when they sing your praises publicly but you love it when they slip a love note into your coat pocket or bag, tell them.

- Do choose carefully when, where, and how you tell them your preferences. If you find it distracting when they whisper sweet words into your ear during intimate moments, wait until later to bring it up. If you love hearing them read their poetry to you in private but are embarrassed at the attention it draws on the subway, wait until you get home to tell them how much you value the personal, private sentiments but that you're not comfortable sharing that intimacy with strangers.

- Do accept their loving expression in the spirit it was offered, without criticism. It doesn't matter how much (or how little) talent they have for putting words together, the important thing is that they love you, and they want you to know. If you're shy about public love talk, find times to be alone together to revel in their loving words. However, if you are a person who is embarrassed by hearing words of love even when it's just the two of you, consider asking them to write it down so that you can read it and reread it any time you need to feel their love.

WHAT SHALL WE TALK ABOUT?

Family Meeting Discussion Openers about Words of Love

Share how you feel about:
1. Giving words of love to your partner
2. Receiving words of love from your partner
3. "Infodumping" by sharing your passion with your partner
4. Receiving your partner's "infodumping" about their passion

DATE NIGHT THEME

Infodump Love Fest

For this date night, you will need a timer, visual timer, or timing app on your phone. Each of you will get a turn to infodump about

Chapter 4: Loving Words

whatever you want to talk about. Decide together how long to make the sessions, and decide who will go first. Then set the timer, and that person gets to talk about their passion, or what happened at work, or whatever they like.

When it's your turn to talk, go for it. You don't need to worry about whether you're talking too much. Until the timer goes off, the stage is yours, and you can feel free to infodump to your heart's delight.

When it's your turn to be the listening partner, do not say a word. This is your loved one's turn to lecture uninterrupted, not a back-and-forth conversation. You can show your interest by orienting your body toward them; this lets them know that you're engaged. If you don't like to look at eyes, just point your face in their direction and look at their forehead or something nearby. It's great to react nonverbally, such as by nodding when you agree or hear something you like.

The only case where it might be appropriate to cut an infodump short is if the speaker is getting overly wound up and emotionally charged as they go around in circles about an upsetting thing that happened. It is not helpful to keep harping on past injustices and injuries. If talking about a previous hurt makes you feel better afterward, then it can be helpful. However, if when you talk about it you feel angrier and angrier, and you find yourself shouting or pacing rather than feeling a sense of completion or acceptance, then the infodumping session should be stopped. At least call for a cooling-off time-out. Next time, choose an interest to infodump about rather than a past grievance.

If spiraling into extreme negativity is something that has happened with you or your partner before, or if it is easy to see that this could happen, then discuss in advance what the rules will be about calling a time out. Here are some possible rules to consider.

When to Call for an Infodump Time-Out

1. The speaker shouts, yells, or criticizes their partner.
2. The speaker paces or stims rapidly as if they are angry or upset, as opposed to the way they pace or stim when they are excited.
3. The speaker appears to be agitated and the agitation is increasing rather than decreasing.
4. .The speaker ignores the timer when their turn is over and keeps talking.

If one of those red flags is present, the listener should use a pre-determined nonverbal signal, such as holding flat hands in a T position for Time-Out. That's the cue for the speaker to stop talking, sit down if they've been pacing, take a few deep breaths, and/or practice relaxation techniques. If infodumping regularly escalates into anger regularly, it's time to find a counselor who is a specialist in relationships, such as one who is Gottman-trained.

Chapter 4: Loving Words

Look for someone who is neurodiversity-affirming. Working with a counselor can help if you keep repeating the same argument again and again.

Do not use the Time-Out signal simply because you are bored, or you've heard this story before, or you're not interested in the topic and want a break from it. If you become bored easily, take that into account when deciding as a couple how long to make each infodumping session. Remember, this is your beloved whom you have chosen above all others. It is a gift of love to listen to their infodump even if you think it's boring. You'll have your turn, and your sweetheart will listen to you, too.

FICTIONAL COUPLES FIXING MIXED SIGNALS

Trish & Bill

Bill sighed contentedly as he sat in front of the television cuddling his fiancée—no, his wife! Trish was his wife now. He sighed again at the thought, a deep sigh filled with love as deep as the ocean, as high as the sky, as something as the something else. There really should be three things, but he didn't want to think about cliches right now.

"Are you okay?" Trish asked.

"Okay? I'm great! I just married the girl of my dreams. How could life be better than this?"

Relating While Autistic

"You just seemed to be sighing a lot. I wanted to be sure you're not sad. Sometimes people sigh because they're sad, you know."

"I am the opposite of sad," Bill said, giving her a squeeze. "It's just that sometimes I love you so much, it's all I can do to keep from saying it out loud."

"Why shouldn't you say it out loud? We've been married for hours. I hope you're not taking me for granted already." She smiled and gave him a kiss when she noticed his stricken look. "I'm kidding."

"Thank goodness," said Bill. "I hope I never take you for granted. I waited a long time for the perfect woman, and I don't want to mess it up now."

"Then, why don't you want to tell me you love me, right out loud? You shouldn't have to censor yourself."

"But I know it embarrasses you."

"What gave you that idea?"

"Well, remember that time we were out for dinner with your family, and I said I loved you? You turned red and looked at your plate and didn't say another word for the rest of the meal. I don't ever want you to feel uncomfortable, even if it means I have to censor myself to keep from telling you I love you all the time."

"Oh, now I remember," Trish said. "We were at that nice restaurant with my parents, and when the waiter asked if

Chapter 4: Loving Words

everything was okay, you said everything was wonderful and that you were in love with me."

"That was all true. But it embarrassed you so much, I've been trying to keep it to myself since then."

"But I wasn't embarrassed that you said you loved me. I was embarrassed because you said it to the waiter, in front of everyone, and people turned and stared at us."

"You mean, I can tell you I love you when we're alone, but not when we're out and about?"

"I love to hear you say you love me, and I love telling you that I love you. I just feel like it's private."

"What a relief." Bill sighed again. "I was having a hard time not telling you how much I adore you."

"I adore you, too, and I love talking about it, just between us."

For Bill, understanding that Trish was embarrassed by his loving words in public, but that she enjoyed exchanging loving words in private, was important.

Justin & Maggie

Justin and Maggie sat down at the table for their weekly Family Meeting. They each had a glass of mango iced tea, and they had prepared guacamole and chips, which were waiting for them in the living room. As soon as their meeting was over, they would binge-watch their favorite series. It gave them something to look forward to, since Family Meetings were not always the most fun. Still, they both knew they needed a regular check-in on the state of the relationship to keep it healthy and to avoid chronic misunderstandings. This time, Maggie started.

"Do you remember when you said you would compliment me more often?"

"Absolutely. I love you, I think you're hot, and you deserve to know that."

"Well, when were you planning to start?"

"Start what?"

"You know, start complimenting me. Last week you said you would do that. Regularly."

"And I absolutely will."

"I believe you. I'm just asking when. A week has gone by, and you haven't said anything nice to me, until just now when you said I'm hot."

"You are hot."

"But all week, you haven't said a single complimentary word to me. I already told you how I felt about that, how much those little words mean to me, and you said you'd change."

Justin sat for a moment thinking. He had intended to compliment Maggie. He had a heart full of so many things he loved about her. Why couldn't he come out and say them? What was stopping him? Finally he broke the awkward silence.

Chapter 4: Loving Words

"I'm embarrassed."

"You're embarrassed to compliment me?"

"No, I'm embarrassed that I don't know how. I don't know what kinds of things you want to hear. I don't know when or how often you want me to say them. I don't know if they should all be spoken or if they could be in writing." Justin kept his eyes down. "I'm mostly embarrassed because I assume that most men know all this stuff already, and if I have to ask you to teach me how, it won't count."

"It won't count?"

"You know, it won't feel like a real compliment if you have to remind me to do it."

Maggie smiled. "A year ago, if a friend of mine had told me they had to remind their boyfriend to say nice things to them, I would have told her to dump the guy."

Justin looked up, terror in his eyes.

"No, don't worry, I'm not going to dump you. I'm just noticing how far we've come since learning about your autism. Now, it makes sense that you would want more direction. Subtle, vague hints like 'Compliment me more' are not your communication style."

"That's for sure. I love structure, quantifying things, like *What, When, How*." He smiled at her. "I've got the *Who* and *Why* part figured out."

Relating While Autistic

Maggie smiled back. "Well, those are the most important parts. How about we come up with ideas together? Can you make yourself a schedule on your phone to remind you?"

"Yes, absolutely!"

The two of them made some notes:

What to compliment, such as commenting on her appearance when she gets dressed up for a special occasion and complimenting a meal when it's her turn to cook.

When to say something nice, such as setting an alarm on his phone to remind himself to communicate his love or compliment Maggie at least once a day.

How to communicate these loving words. Sometimes he will speak loving words, such as when she gets all dressed up or when she cooks dinner. Sometimes he will text a quick "I love you" or a heart emoji during a break in his work day. He might draw a heart or XOX on a sticky note or write a loving phrase on a greeting card when there's a particular occasion.

Justin made a note to himself to create a list of all the things he loved about Maggie so he could rotate through them and avoid repeating himself too often. He was afraid this would take all the romance out of it, but Maggie assured him that the fact that he was willing to go to all this effort made it even more romantic.

Soon the list was done. There was nothing else on their agenda, so they took their tea to the living room for an evening of chips and guac and loving talk.

Chapter 4: Loving Words

Lucia & Naima

Lucia and Naima had decided that, rather than have a weekly Family Meeting as many couples do, they would have a couple's book club with just the two of them. They'd drink wine, munch on appetizers, and discuss the book they had read. It was a fun way to learn more about each other and what made them tick as a couple.

The first book they decided to read together was Gary Chapman's *The 5 Love Languages*. It gave them a lot to think and talk about. When it came to the chapter on words of affirmation, they realized that they were already on the same page. They each loved to tell each other how they felt and to hear words of love reflected back to them. Their comfort zone included spoken and written language when they were alone together. In public, and with people they were less familiar with, they often struggled with social communication, but when they were alone together, all the barriers seemed to melt away.

Crow & Daisy

DAISY: (*Out of the blue*) So, I read this article online about communication.

CROW: Smooth segue.

DAISY: I don't segue. No seg, no way.

CROW: Okay. So, you read an article.

DAISY: It's all about couples and communication.

Relating While Autistic

CROW: We're not a couple.

DAISY: Disagree. Anyway, I figured out something about us.

CROW: There's no us.

DAISY: Here's what I figured out. One of my strongest love languages is Words of Affirmation.

CROW: Words of Affirmation?

DAISY: You know, like saying nice things that make someone feel good.

CROW: I do know what affirmation means. So, does this mean you like to give people these words of affirmation, or you wish people would give them to you?

DAISY: For me it's both. I love hearing nice things, you know, compliments and that kind of thing. But I also like to tell the people I love (*coughs "you"*) how I feel.

CROW: I must be a huge disappointment. How can you bear it?

DAISY: The way I bear all things. Like a badass.

CROW: So, I guess, if I want to be a good friend to you—

DAISY: Which you do.

CROW: If I want to be a friend to you, I should say something nice every once in a while, right?

DAISY: That would be delightful.

CROW: I don't know what you want to hear. I mean, I do have feelings. For one, I feel protective of you. You're such an innocent.

Chapter 4: Loving Words

DAISY: Hey, I've got lots of experience...points.

CROW: I know you don't need me to take care of you, I'm just telling you how I feel. Or, I'm trying to, but Words of Affirmation is not my proficiency.

DAISY: That's for sure. What's your Charisma score, 5?

CROW: I'd have to roll high for persuasion if I wanted to say something nice. And I'm not that lucky with dice.

DAISY: Maybe today is your day. Let's pretend I just handed you my lucky dice. What nice thing would you want to say to me if you rolled a 20 for initiative?

CROW: (*thinks for a moment*) I'd say that being with you makes me feel like I roll a 20 every time I pick up the dice. A day that starts with one of your ridiculous "G'morning" gifs is a good day for me. Every night I need to hear you say "G'night, sweet dreams," before I can fall asleep. I'd tell you that you're my very best friend and I can't imagine what my life would be without you in it. But like I said, words are not my power.

DAISY: Wow. When you roll a 20, you sure know what to do with it.

CROW: Then I hope you recorded that because you may never hear it again.

DAISY: Oh, I recorded it all right. It will go down in the annals of my memory as the day that Crow said, "I love you."

Relating While Autistic

CROW: Wait, I didn't—

DAISY: (*puts a hand over Crow's mouth*) Too late, you said it, I heard it, you couldn't deny it if you tried with both hands. To thine own elf be true, Crow. And don't worry, I love you, too. You are the chaotic-neutral half-elf cleric of my heart.

THEY SAY

As an autistic married to someone with ADHD, we are info-dumping experts! Normally we're both excited to hear about the other person's interests, even if it's not something we're super interested in, because it makes them happy. But in the times where we just don't have the capacity for all of it, we've learned to communicate that right now we need a little less dissertation on WWI battleships (him) or the Eurovision Song Contest (me). It might be because we have other things we'd like or need to talk about, or maybe we just need extra quiet at the moment. The important thing is to let each other know.

— Tara, autistic woman married to a man with ADHD

I infodump to her all the time. She will listen to it for a bit, but when I don't stop, she politely tells me that she is done listening about

Chapter 4: Loving Words

my special interest or current fascination right now. I sometimes cannot keep it bottled up and later in the day I continue to infodump right where I left off, and then I get a little more stern talking-to about it. She will try her hardest to be nice and tell me that she loves that I like that topic, but she doesn't really have the same care for it and would like for me to stop infodumping her so much.

— Thomas McDonald III

Infodumping? Haha! Sometimes he tunes me out. I talk way too much! Like the motor in my mouth is much speedier than the motor in my brain. By the time my brain catches up, my mouth has put out way too much information. He never shames me for it, though; he just lets me ramble for a while and I get the thoughts or feelings out. Sometimes I'm scared that the things I say will make him stop loving me, but for some reason he never goes away.

— Wendy B.

Chapter 5

Loving Touch

"Too often we underestimate the power of a touch, a smile, a kind word, a listening ear, an honest compliment, or the smallest act of caring, all of which have the potential to turn a life around."

— Leo Buscaglia, *Love*

Chapter 5: Loving Touch

Loving touch is one way many couples communicate their affection. This is the language that Gary Chapman calls "Physical Touch." Like any form of communication, loving touch can be expressive and receptive.

Expressive loving touch includes such things as reaching out to take your beloved's hand, stroking their hair, and offering a hug or kiss. People with this expressive language may be considered "touchy-feely," and it's great if their partner appreciates this kind of touch.

Receptive loving touch describes people who love it when their partner reaches out to touch them. They find being in physical contact with their loved one can recharge their batteries.

It's important to be aware of how your partner feels about touching and being touched. Many people startle easily, and having their partner come up behind them to surprise them with a hug may trigger a "fight or flight or freeze" reflex. If they freeze, their partner may not realize that they dislike unexpected touch, and unless they are told, they will probably keep on reaching out to touch them. On the other hand, if they respond to unexpected touch by "fight or flight," they may unintentionally punch their beloved or break away and put distance between them. The partner who unwittingly caused this reaction in an attempt to show affection may feel rejected or wonder if their partner really loves them.

Relating While Autistic

Some people crave firm touch, and a hand softly caressing their own hand may make them startle, cringe, or want to shake it off. Others may find a firm touch like a hearty handshake or big hug to be actually painful and prefer a more gentle contact. Either way, knowing what your partner likes and dislikes is important.

It's so important to talk with your partner about how you feel about touch. Do you love touching and being touched by your partner when you are in a calm state and it's not a surprise? Tell your beloved. Are there parts of your body that are too sensitive or ticklish to be touched, that you wish your partner would avoid? Be clear with them. No one wants to accidentally send their sweetheart into a sensory overload or meltdown. Perhaps in the presence of sensory or social stressors you might feel that you cannot be touched at all, but any other time it's okay. Let your partner know. Knowledge of how each one of you feels about loving touches, whether expressive or receptive, will go a long way toward heading off potential misunderstandings.

Amy Schaber calls one of the Neurodivergent Love Languages "Please Crush My Soul Back into My Body." This refers to proprioceptive needs, or the desire for deep pressure. Many NDs find it calming and restorative to feel squeezed or weighed down under a blanket. If you've seen the 2010 HBO movie *Temple Grandin*, you probably remember the squeeze machine she constructed for herself when she was eighteen. It was very effective in helping her

Chapter 5: Loving Touch

calm down when she was anxious or overwhelmed. You may not need a machine, but if you do, the internet will provide plans for building your own, Many people find that wearing compression garments or a vest that is a size too small provides a squeezing effect that helps them relax. Others like the feeling of a weighted blanket, wearable weights, or having a large dog lean against them or their partner give them a bear hug. For some people, simply lying down flat on a hard floor, with their whole body in contact with the surface, provides relief from tension and a feeling of being grounded. When you're in a loving neurodivergent relationship, you can ask your partner for a long, deep pressure hug to "crush your soul back into your body."

 ## RED LIGHT/GREEN LIGHT TIPS
FOR LOVING TOUCH

 RED LIGHT: Your partner sometimes shrinks away from your touch when you're in an affectionate mood.

 Green Lights:

- Do refrain from touching them in that moment, and give them some time before talking about it or touching them again.

Relating While Autistic

- Do remember that you are loved by your beloved, and don't assume they don't want you to ever touch them again, or that they don't love you anymore.
- Do remember that an aversion to touch may be temporary and could be caused by many things that have nothing to do with you, such as sensory overwhelm, or a bad day at work, or stress of any kind.
- Do be mature about it, rather than pouting or trying to punish your partner by withholding your love. You can go on loving them just as much even if you're not expressing it through loving touch right now.
- Do ask them, when they seem calm and receptive, about their reaction to your touch. Perhaps your touch was too firm, or too soft or tickly, or something else was bothering them. It's not always about you.

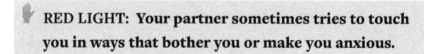

RED LIGHT: Your partner sometimes tries to touch you in ways that bother you or make you anxious.

Green Lights:

- Do tell them how you feel about being touched like that. You have a right to your body, and if you're not in the mood to be touched for any reason, or no reason at

Chapter 5: Loving Touch

all, that's okay.

- Do let them know what it was about this particular touch that bothered you. Were they touching you in public in a way that made you uncomfortable? Was their touch too light or too firm, or on a part of your body that you don't want touched? Everyone has a right to bodily autonomy, and it is perfectly fine to say that your toes, or ears, or any part of your body, is off limits. That doesn't mean you don't love them, and their respect for you will be evident when they comply with your rules about your body.
- Do be clear about your feelings. You can't assume that they should know how you feel. No matter how much your partner loves you or how well they know you, they still can't read your mind.

WHAT SHALL WE TALK ABOUT, WHAT SHALL WE DO?

Family Meeting Activity

You might have a discussion about how you like to touch and be touched. This is always a good way to continue learning about your loved one. But what if, instead of having a discussion about touch, you played a game? You may remember the childhood game, "Mother, May I?" In this game everyone lines up at a starting line, and one person, the designated "Mother," stands at the end goal. "Mother" calls a child by name and gives them an instruction, such as, "Please take 2 giant steps forward," or "Please take 1 tiny step forward." The child must say, "Mother, may I?" and when "Mother" replies, "Yes, you may," the child takes the specified steps toward the finish line.

Your new version of this game is "Lover, May I?" Each of you take turns giving your partner directions on what part of your body you want them to touch, and in what way, such as, "Lover, please touch my forehead, softly." This is followed by the response, "Lover, may I?" and the permission, "Yes, you may." In this way you may learn a lot about where and how your beloved likes to be touched.

And you thought Family Meetings were going to be boring.

Chapter 5: Loving Touch

DATE NIGHT THEME

Blindfolded Date

This is an "at home" date night, on an evening when you can have privacy and not be interrupted. If you have children, arrange for them to have a sleepover with friends or relatives.

Choose an activity that you both enjoy doing together, only this time, you will be blindfolded. You might eat or feed each other dessert blindfolded or take a bath together. You could take turns preparing a snack or following a recipe with one of you blindfolded and the other providing verbal and hand-over-hand guidance.

Two important things to be aware of on blindfolded date night are safety and comfort. If either of you feels anxious about any aspect of the activity, don't do it.

For reasons of safety, make sure the blindfolds are not too tight and are easy to take off if you need to see or if either of you becomes uneasy while blindfolded. Don't try to walk blindfolded or do anything potentially dangerous. It's better to ditch the blindfolds altogether if it's uncomfortable for either one of you. You could just keep your eyes closed with the freedom to peek any time you want or need to, and then close your eyes again when you feel comfortable doing so. This activity is about having fun with touch without using sight, but you can still have fun even if you decide to keep your eyes open the whole time. Remember, your date night is yours, and you get to make the rules together.

FICTIONAL COUPLES

Trish & Bill

At one of their Family Meetings, Trish said she wanted to bring something up, but then she fell silent and blushed, and words wouldn't come. Finally, after some patient waiting and a certain amount of coaxing and guessing on Bill's part, she admitted that she wanted to ask Bill why he no longer did one of the things he used to do in their intimate times together.

He told her that he stopped doing that because she didn't like it when he did that. This came as a surprise to Trish, because she did, in fact, enjoy the activity quite a bit. In reconstructing their recent history, they realized that one morning when they were being intimate, she had seemed to rebuff some of his advances, and he had decided he must stop doing that. It turned out that she had been worried about getting to work on time and distracted by the clock.

They came to a mutually agreeable understanding about when they would be both be comfortable engaging in various

Chapter 5: Loving Touch

aspects of their lovemaking. Trish realized that, even though it was difficult for her to talk about some private things even with Bill, it was important to make herself share her feelings. Bill realized that he shouldn't make assumptions about how Trish feels about something based on a single incident. They were both grateful they had set up regular Family Meetings to improve and open up their communication...

Justin & Maggie

Justin was flat on his stomach on the kitchen floor when Maggie got home.

"Are you okay?" She looked down at him in concern.

"Yeah. I mean, no, but yeah." He sighed. "I just had a crappy day today."

"I'm sorry, babe. Is there anything I can do?"

Justin lifted his head and looked up at her. "Seriously?"

"Of course! Just let me know what would help you feel better."

"Would you lie down on top of me?"

"You mean, right here on the floor? Won't that hurt you?"

"It won't hurt, and I think it would make me feel better. I just feel like I want to be squashed down into the floor."

"Okay, here goes," said Maggie as she took off her shoes and started to lie down on him. "If this is a come-on line, it's a weird one, even for you."

Relating While Autistic

Justin chuckled softly. "No, I'm not trying to start something. I just need to feel weight on my whole body, and you're human-sized. And heated."

Giggling, Maggie lowered herself onto his body. "Human-sized and heated. Maybe I should add that to my resume."

Justin exhaled, and Maggie could feel him relax under the weight of her body. He breathed slowly and deeply and seemed to almost melt into the floor. After a couple of minutes he thanked her, and she stood up.

"Did that really help?" she asked.

"Yeah, it helped a lot." Justin stood up too. "I've been reading about autistic people who use squeeze machines or other deep pressure things. They say it really helps them reduce stress and anxiety, and I'm sold. That felt great!"

"Well, I'm here for you, babe. Any time you need a heated human-sized weight, just ask."

For Justin, asking Maggie for the deep pressure he needed was awkward at first, but it turned out to be a great stress-relieving strategy.

Lucia & Naima

"Are you mad at me?" Lucia asked.

"What do you think?" Naima said frostily.

"I don't know, that's why I'm asking. You seem distant."

Chapter 5: Loving Touch

"Oh, you think *I* seem distant? That's a good one!" Naima's voice rose a bit. "You're the queen of distance, but you think *I'm* the distant one."

Lucia was confused. "Naima, I love you. I don't feel distant from you, but I feel like you're giving me the cold shoulder and I don't know why."

"When I tried to hold your hand and you pulled it away, that really hurt me. Why did you do that?"

"Oh, yeah, now I know what you're talking about. We were in the lobby of the movie theater, and I saw someone I used to work with. She was looking right at us like she was about to say hi, and then you grabbed my hand and I was embarrassed."

"Embarrassed?" Naima was shocked. "Are you ashamed of our love?"

"I'm not, but there are a lot of homophobic people out there. I read about all the hate crimes." Lucia shrugged. "And, I guess I don't want to give people something to gossip about. That person I saw loves to talk about people behind their backs."

"Are you really worried about hate crimes or gossip if people know we're a couple?" Naima looked crestfallen. "Or is that just an excuse because you don't love me anymore?"

"How can you say that?"

"Because you pulled away from me like I had COVID and you were my grandmother."

Relating While Autistic

"I'm just not as comfortable with PDA as you are. It makes me feel awkward, like everyone is looking at me, and I hate that. But when we're alone or somewhere semi-private like a restaurant booth or inside the movie theater, I love holding hands and being affectionate with you. I adore you, Naima."

"I didn't think about how you might feel about touching in public. I'm so happy and proud to be with you and I want the world to know, but I do know you don't like people staring at you. I'll try to control my impulse to reach out and touch you when we're in public."

"As long as you don't try to control that impulse when we're alone together. I love it when you touch me, and I always will." Lucia reached out and took Naima's hand. "Thanks for understanding."

"Always happy to learn more about you."

For Lucia and Naima, it was important to understand that there are times and places when touch is less welcome but that loving touch when alone is a welcome part of their relationship.

Daisy & Crow

DAISY: So, you like cuddling, right?

CROW: Why do you assume I like cuddling?

DAISY: Because we're cuddling right now, we've been cuddling since we started watching TV, and you haven't pulled

Chapter 5: Loving Touch

away from me, clutching your pearls, crying, "Unhand me, you fiend!"

CROW: Maybe I'm just cuddling with you for warmth.

DAISY: It's August.

CROW: Oh, all right, I don't find cuddling with you at all repulsive.

DAISY: You love it. And you also love it when we hold hands, and when we hug and kiss every time we say hello or good-bye.

CROW: Where are you going with this?

DAISY: I'm just wondering if you're an Ace of Hearts or an Ace of Clubs.

CROW: You lost me there.

DAISY: That's okay, you'll catch up, and it will be totally worth the trip when you do. You find my non-sequiturs charming.

CROW: Borderline charming.

DAISY: I'll take it. So, I've been reading about asexual folx online. Some of them actually enjoy sex with their loved one when they have it, but they never miss it or want it between times. I call those Aces of Hearts. Then others hate the idea of sex and never want to do it at all. I call those the Aces of Clubs, because they would club someone over the head before they'd have sex with them.

CROW: Yeah, I get that. Interesting.

DAISY: So, which are you, an Ace of Hearts or an Ace of Clubs?

CROW: It's not that simple.

Relating While Autistic

DAISY: It's not that complicated. Are you a virgin? Have you ever had sex? Follow-up question: If you did have sex, did you ever enjoy it?

CROW: No, I am not a virgin, I have had sex when I was with someone. Yes, I enjoyed it at the time. The problem is not whether I would enjoy it; it's that it always leads to people being disappointed, or hurt, or angry. Life is just simpler without relationships and the expectations that go along with them. Hence, we are not in a relationship.

DAISY: Hard disagree. We are in a relationship, but I love your use of "hence," you literate charmer.

CROW: I'm serious, Daisy. If we were to start a sexual relationship, which we're not, it would end up with you being hurt, and thinking I don't love you or that I don't find you attractive. People get tired of always having to be the one to initiate sex, and it's not a fair position to put anyone in. It's easier and kinder if I just avoid romantic entanglements of every ilk.

DAISY: Ilk! Be still, my heart!

CROW: Exactly. Be still, your heart. Get out now and save yourself.

DAISY: Did it never occur to you that I might prefer a relationship where I only have sex when I want to, and I never have to worry about being coerced or forced?

CROW: Has anyone ever forced you to have sex with them?

Chapter 5: Loving Touch

DAISY: I'm an autistic woman in a neurotypical male world. My ability to discern whether someone's intentions are honorable or evil is practically nil. I tend to trust everyone, and that's a position that can end badly.

CROW: Names. I want names. I will seriously hurt them.

DAISY: No. The past is past, I've had a lot of therapy, and I'm okay. The only reason I even bring it up is to let you see how much I would appreciate having an Ace of Hearts in my life, rather than a misogynistic, entitled, cisgender, heterosexual male.

CROW: I hate that those things happened to you. You don't deserve to be hurt or used.

DAISY: I know that now, too. I didn't deserve that. I do deserve to be happy, and you make me happy, Crow.

CROW: (*Cuddling her closer*) I'm glad. You make me happy, too, weirdo.

DAISY: I know.

CROW: So, does this mean you want to have sex?

DAISY: Not today. Not tomorrow. But someday. I'll let you know.

And, when the time was right for them both, she did just that.

Relating While Autistic

THEY SAY

I don't mind touch as much as some may. If I am overstimulated, though, and I get touched, I will just say, "Please, no." This can cause her some confusion if I don't tell her I'm having issues, and she may feel like she did something wrong or that I am mad. It helps when I can tell her I'm overstimulated.

— Thomas McDonald III

When Elliot and I first got married, I worked at a hip tech company with an open plan office in downtown San Francisco. Open plan did not work for me. By 11:00 AM I was completely spent, unable to do anything except stare at the computer and wait for the day to end. I'd go into the bathroom and sit with my back pressed against the cool tile or put rain music on my headphones and practice deep breathing. Nothing helped. At 5:00 PM I'd drive the hour home and crawl into bed. Elliot would arrive to find me wrapped up in a blanket burrito.

"Do you want me to lay on you?" he'd ask.

"Yes please."

I'd open up the blanket and unfurl myself and he'd lay his whole body weight on top of me. The air would rush out of my lungs in one big heave, and with it went the open plan office and the fluorescent lights and the honking cars and the constant

Chapter 5: Loving Touch

conversation and the traffic. The itchy feeling along my skin that had grown and spread all day was snuffed out. I felt safe again, and just a little more functional.

— Marian, first shared in *Dating While Autistic*

by W. W. Marsh

Chapter 6

Loving Gifts

"No one has ever become poor by giving."

— Anne Frank

"For it is in giving that we receive."

— Francis of Assisi

Chapter 6: Loving Gifts

Everyone likes receiving gifts.

Except when they don't.

It may seem obvious that gifts are good, but not everyone feels the same way about giving and receiving presents. Some people have a history of stress surrounding gift-giving events.

People who highly value honesty may have been encouraged to lie as children, saying that they loved presents that they actually hated. Now the very act of opening presents brings up past internal conflicts. Their inner yearning for complete honesty is at odds with the struggle to say the "socially appropriate" thing that people expect.

Some have obsessed over giving the perfect gift but have failed to achieve perfection every time. The burden of self-disappointment can be a heavy load to bear.

Others have become weary of opening well-intended gifts of polyester shirts and fancy perfume, but they don't know how to tell their loved ones that they cannot touch polyester and they can't abide the smell of artificial perfumes, no matter how elegant or expensive.

Many remember painfully the noisy, crowded, chaotic birthday parties of childhood, with kids running around, balloons popping, the smell of the burning candles, the idea of the birthday child blowing germs all over the cake, and, worst of all, the dreaded Surprise Party. Who wants to walk into a dark room and have a bunch of people jump out and yell?

Of course, not everyone feels the same way about gift-giving and -receiving. Some people feel especially loved and cared for when their partner brings them little things, a flower, their favorite bagel, or something they saw that reminded them of their love. Some people adore giving things to their beloved as personal, tangible symbols of their deep feelings. It doesn't have to be expensive, because it really is the thought that makes the gift special.

In *The 5 Love Languages*, Gary Chapman calls this language Receiving Gifts. It's not a mercenary thing so much as it is one more way of demonstrating love. It means a lot when a partner takes the time to find something personal, something their beloved can hold and keep, reminding them of the love they share even when they're apart.

The corresponding ND Love Language created by Amythest Schaber is "I found this cool rock/button/leaf/etc. and thought you would like it." Autistic partners understand that sometimes things people in the neuromajority might find odd would make the perfect gift. If your partner loves watching geese fly overhead and stops to look up until the last straggler has flown out of sight, then a realistic plastic goose as a gift shows that you get them. If

Chapter 6: Loving Gifts

you know your beloved is fascinated by spiders and spiderwebs, then a photograph of a spiderweb glistening with dewdrops at sunrise will delight them. However, if your partner hates spiders, it won't matter how beautiful the pattern is, they won't like it if there's an arachnid at the center of it. Remember, it's not about what you, yourself, find beautiful and fascinating; it's about your loved one. Look at the world through their eyes, and you'll notice the things that bring them joy.

RED LIGHT/GREEN LIGHT TIPS FOR LOVING GIFTS

 RED LIGHT: Your beloved gives you the same present every year. You loved it when they surprised you with a beautiful Christmas sweater in your first holiday season together, but now you have a closet full of sweaters you only wear in December.

 Green Lights:
- Do accept the gift with gratitude rather than criticism. After all, you loved it the first time, and it's clear they want to keep making you happy by recreating that first wonderful holiday as a couple.

Relating While Autistic

- Do communicate directly rather than hinting. Subtle hints are often missed or misunderstood.
- Do let them know that you have loved every sweater they gave you but that there aren't enough days in December to wear them all. Suggest that it might be time for a new tradition and go shopping together, in person or online, to point out things you would love to own in the same price range.

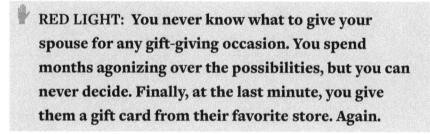

RED LIGHT: **You never know what to give your spouse for any gift-giving occasion. You spend months agonizing over the possibilities, but you can never decide. Finally, at the last minute, you give them a gift card from their favorite store. Again.**

Green Lights:

- Do commit to doing something different rather than giving gift cards forever. Consider asking them or one of their friends or family members for gift suggestions. You want your partner to feel special and to know that you took time to find something they'd like. The gift card doesn't show how much time you spent thinking about their gift; it looks like you were being lazy, which isn't true. You just need guidance to find something more personal.

Chapter 6: Loving Gifts

• Do go shopping together, either in person or on the internet, especially if your partner doesn't need to be surprised. Let them pick out what they want themselves, but then you hide it and wrap it so they can open it up.

WHAT SHALL WE TALK ABOUT?

Family Meeting Discussion Openers about Loving Gifts

Ask and answer any or all of these questions, taking turns with your partner:

1. What do you like about giving gifts? About receiving gifts?
2. What do you dislike about giving gifts? About receiving gifts?
3. What do you feel is a good range of how much to spend on each other for birthdays and other holidays? Can you find a happy medium amount you both feel comfortable with, and stick to it?
4. Would you rather put your money together and spend it on a trip or something large for the household?
5. Do you prefer to be surprised or do you want to know what's in the gift bags and boxes to avoid suspense and stress?

DATE NIGHT THEME

Sharing Wish Lists

This could be an at-home date in front of a fireplace or a fireplace video on the television. Take turns sharing wish lists of things you might like to receive. You may also make wish lists of things the two of you want as a couple, such as a vacation, car, or appliance. Since this is a date night, keep it light and fanciful. If you find that either one of you feels stressed out by the discussion, for example, if it triggers worry about finances, then drop the discussion. Choose something else to do instead, such as watching a movie or reading out loud to each other from a favorite book.

FICTIONAL COUPLES

Trish & Bill

As their first anniversary approached, Trish started to worry about what to give Bill. It had to be perfect. He was the perfect husband and deserved the perfect gift, something intimate and romantic. But what was it? What did women give their husbands? Socks and underwear? He probably needed them because he rarely thought about buying such things for himself, but no. It was intimate

Chapter 6: Loving Gifts

without being at all romantic. Tools? TV commercials showed men happily receiving tools, but Bill had never mentioned wanting them. She didn't want to imply that she thought he should be handier around the house. Trish was at a loss, so she brought it up at their next Family Meeting.

"Bill, I've been thinking about anniversary presents."

"Me, too! What do you want? Anything at all. As you know, I'm generally clueless, so all clues are appreciated."

"No, I was thinking about what I would give you for our anniversary."

"Wives give husbands anniversary gifts? I thought it was just husbands giving gifts to their wives."

"That wouldn't be fair. But I don't know what you want."

"I don't need anything except you. But I've been going round and round in my head over what to give you. You're the perfect wife, and you deserve the perfect gift."

"Would you like to go shopping together sometime, and I'll show you what I like?" Trish offered.

"For you, I'd even go shopping, my darling." He took her hand and kissed it.

"Hmm. Sounds like it wouldn't be fun for you. How about online shopping? We can go on Etsy, and I'll show you all the things I like and you can choose one for me."

"Or you can tell me which one you like best, and I'll get that one."

Relating While Autistic

Trish giggled. "Yes, that sounds even better. I'll choose it, you buy it and wrap it, and I'll be thrilled to receive it."

"About the wrapping part ..."

"Two words: gift bags."

"I think I can manage that." Bill looked visibly relieved.

"But what about my gift to you?" Trish asked.

"You don't have to give me anything, really."

"Oh, but I just this minute thought of the perfect thing! You'll love it!"

Bill looked uneasy. "You know I don't love surprises ..."

"Right. I'll tell you: a gift certificate for ebooks or audio books."

Bill felt happy as a lark in springtime, as a clam at high tide, as a pig in clover, as a husband about to be given the gift of books he wouldn't have to find shelf space for. "That would be perfect! Thank you!"

For Trish and Bill, knowing in advance exactly what to give each other and what they would receive washed away the stress of gift-giving and receiving like a cleansing storm of cliches.

Justin & Maggie

"What do you want for Christmas?" Maggie asked one Saturday evening while they scrolled through movies, deciding what to watch.

"I don't know. I never know. Why are you asking now?"

Chapter 6: Loving Gifts

"There are so many holiday specials, it put me in the mood."

"Those Christmas specials are there all year long, you know."

"I know, but now it's actually the right time for them. So, do you have any hints for me?"

"I hate hints. Can we just skip the whole gift-giving thing? It's so stressful!"

Maggie thought about this for a while. "So, I get that you don't want to try to think of things you want and then try to act surprised. And you don't want to try to think of what I might want and then stress over whether I'll like it or not."

"Exactly! You know me so well."

"Here's an idea. What if we gave each other experiences rather than things?"

"I'm intrigued."

"Like, we could give each other season tickets to the local theater, or memberships to a museum, or the aquarium."

"Brilliant! Let's go online right now and get it over with!" He pulled his tablet onto his lap and opened it.

"Get it over with?" Maggie raised an eyebrow.

"I mean, let's enjoy the magic that is holiday giving right this very minute. So we won't have to think about it again for a year."

Maggie chuckled. "Okay, let's do it, then."

And they did.

Relating While Autistic

Lucia & Naima

Because their birthdays were in the same month, Lucia and Naima always celebrated together. It was almost like Christmas in August, and they loved it. They had pre-determined amounts to spend on each other, and they both knew each other well enough to know what they would like. They had just been to the *Supernatural* convention, so that was the theme of their gift giving.

Naima loved watching Lucia open the T-shirt of Misha Collins as his angelic character, Castiel, wearing his iconic trench coat with wings outspread. She loved watching her try it on, too. It was a perfect fit.

Then she opened her gift and saw a framed poster of *Supernatural*, signed by the cast members. There was a certificate of authentication on the back. It was amazing. Also, amazingly expensive. Naima felt her stomach drop and go cold.

"Why?" She searched for words. "How?" She took a deep breath and tried again. "We agreed on how much we'd spend, Lucia. I know how much this cost. Why did you break our agreement?"

"But I couldn't resist! I knew how much you'd love it, and it'll look great in our apartment." Lucia's smile started to fade. "Don't you like it?"

"Of course, I love it, but now I feel like a jerk, opening up this, when all I gave you was a stupid T-shirt!"

"I love this shirt!"

Chapter 6: Loving Gifts

"Well, do you love making me look bad? Do you love making me lose trust in you? We made an agreement, and you broke it." Naima closed her eyes. "Have you broken any other promises?"

Lucia was shocked. "No! How can you ask that? I can't believe you're acting like this after I gave you such a great gift!"

"The gift is the problem! Don't you even see that?"

"I see that you don't appreciate a gift I put a lot of thought into.""And a lot of money into."

"I can't even talk to you about this right now. Let's take a break and try again later when we've had a chance to cool off and think."

When they came together later, they each took turns talking about how they felt and listening and reflecting back what they understood their partner felt. It really helped them to see each other's perspective. Lucia came to understand that breaking a promise wasn't worth risking losing Naima's trust. Naima came to understand that Lucia's gift was given from the heart with no cost comparison involved. They both agreed to stick to their gift budget in the future, and if one of them found a perfect gift that cost more, they would talk about it before buying it. It was better to spoil a surprise rather than to break a promise.

Relating While Autistic

Daisy & Crow

It was January, the first new year since Daisy and Crow had become an official couple. Daisy finally learned what Crow had in their pants, but she would never tell anyone, not even under pain of torture. So don't ask. This evening they were cuddling together on the couch, reading.

DAISY: I've been thinking.

CROW: Like ya' do.

DAISY: I'm glad you've been paying attention. So, I've been thinking, like I do, and I've decided this will be The Year of Something Tangible.

CROW: Is that a thing?

DAISY: It is now. I just named it, and naming a thing gives you power over it.

CROW: If you say so.

DAISY: Exactly, you get it. So, this will be The Year of Something Tangible.

CROW: What does that mean? To be more specific, what does that mean for me?

DAISY: In the past year, we have celebrated many things together. It was our collaboration that conquered the mighty dragon Herensuge in our greatest quest. Together we have braved public transportation and attended the D&D convention in a far-off city. We have discovered that true

Chapter 6: Loving Gifts

love is not bound by typical human expectations. We have become a couple, even by your own estimation.

CROW: Acknowledged.

DAISY: Sweet-talker! Now, I know you do not subscribe to society's view of holidays and typical gift-giving occasions.

CROW: Right, it's all made up by the money-grubbing greeting card industry.

DAISY: So you have said. And it's true that all of the experiences that make up our love story are written on my heart, where they can never be erased. But in this Year of Something Tangible, our love will also be written in ink on card stock, placed in an envelope, and mailed.

CROW: Mailed? Like a greeting card, with a stamp, dropped in a mailbox? Seriously?

DAISY: Yes, mailed, as in days of yore. I'm giving you notice. My birthday is in March, and this year, I expect a card.

CROW: Cards are stupid. Why would you want a birthday card?

DAISY: A card is something tangible, something I can hold in my hands and read and re-read. Any time I'm feeling alone, and you're at work or somewhere else, I can bring forth my card and read it again. I'll feel close to you, even when we're apart. And I want one for my birthday.

CROW: You're actually pretty low-maintenance.

DAISY: I'm not a thing to be maintained. I'm a person to be

cherished and appreciated. And I want a birthday card. So gimme!

CROW: Okay, I guess that's not too much to ask. So, what's your address?

DAISY: You know where I live.

CROW: I do, but the post office wants more than the building on the corner across from the park, first apartment at the top of the stairs and straight on to morning. They want numbers, streets, zip codes.

DAISY: I'll write it down for you. Here. And my birthday is March 15.

CROW: I think I can remember the Ides of March. Now, forget about it or it won't be a surprise.

As it turned out, Daisy was completely and utterly surprised to receive a heart-shaped box of chocolates on Valentine's Day from a person who doesn't believe in made-up holidays.

And also a card on her birthday the next month.

Chapter 6: Loving Gifts

THEY SAY

I am a horrible gift-giver. I know it, she knows it. I try to pick out something she'll love in my head, but it isn't anything close to what she had been hinting towards. I can tell you what she's into as a special interest, but when I'm buying a present, the anxiety and disassociation I get have made me choose some weird things. Thankfully, my wife understands that I am different, and her love has always been 100%.

— Thomas McDonald III

We've learned to just ask for what we want or to make lists. Lists need to include either a website link or a brand with size, color, and where to buy it. Receipts are given with each gift, along with the understanding that it's okay to return it. I won't be offended. I want you to enjoy the gift, so my feelings are not hurt if it's wrong somehow and you exchange it for something you do want.

— Wendy B.

Chapter 7

Loving Time

"The bad news is time flies. The good news is you're the pilot."

— Michael Altshuler

"Time is too slow for those who wait, too swift for those who fear... but for those who love, time is eternity."

— Henry Van Dyke

Chapter 7: Loving Time

The gift of time, of your undistracted focus beamed toward your beloved alone, is one of the greatest gifts you can give someone. I once knew a man who asked his wife for two minutes of her undivided attention. She agreed and sat down to hear what he had to say. What he had to say was...nothing. He just looked into her eyes and smiled for a full 120 seconds. Soon she was smiling, too. After the two minutes were up, they each went about the rest of their busy days. It seemed an insignificant way to spend a short amount of time, but I imagine that their step was a bit lighter, their outlook a bit brighter, due to having spent that time together doing absolutely nothing, being absolutely together.

Gary Chapman describes one of the five love languages as Quality Time, expressing your loving feelings through attending to your beloved. A person can spend a lot of "quantity time" adjacent to their partner while also checking their messages, reading a book, or playing a game on their phone. That kind of together time is also pleasant but not necessarily meaningful quality time. Spending even a shorter amount of quality time fully focused on your loved one with nothing else vying for your attention can mean so much.

When couples have children or pets, this can be challenging. There will always be others who also need your time. But remember your priority should be your life partner. Theodore

Relating While Autistic

Hesburgh wrote, "The most important thing a father can do for his children is to love their mother." Of course, we would amend it to apply equally to any and all spouses, and not just children, but four-pawed fur-babies as well. Carving out time for your beloved in your busy life will reap future benefits in the continuing strength of your relationship and family.

Parallel Play is the corresponding Neurodivergent Love Language that Amythest Schaber wrote about. In this language, it's perfectly fine if you're not gazing into each other's eyes. For many, this would be highly uncomfortable, and demanding eye contact would spoil their time together. Continual conversation is not required, either. Being in companionable proximity is meaningful. If one person is reading a book and another is playing a game online but they're on the same couch and feeling secure in the nearness of their loved one, that time can be precious. If a couple chooses to talk about what they're doing or reading, great. If they enjoy convivial, restful silence in one another's presence without a word, wonderful. There are no rules of engagement for parallel play.

A lot of neurodivergent people struggle with time management. Whether they're autistic, or an ADHDer, or an AuDHDer, there are so many ways time can feel like the enemy.

Time management can get in the way of a couple's day-to-day lives. If one or both partners struggle to manage their time

Chapter 7: Loving Time

effectively, it can lead to hurt feelings, missed appointments, and uncertainty.

For some, the issue with time management is Time Comprehension. Their active, creative minds don't easily latch onto the concept of linear time, and knowing the difference between five minutes, an hour, or five hours does not come to them instinctively. How long will it take to wash the dishes, mow the lawn, or get ready to go out on a date? It's a mystery. In a relationship, this can lead to misunderstandings and being late to or even completely missing important events.

Time Planning is another important issue for many. Calendars and schedules look like a minefield of potential failure. If one partner promises to do something at a particular time, and then they're unable to meet that commitment, the stress can be tremendous. Many already live with perfectionism, and the idea of planning for the future, not knowing if you'll be able to follow the plan perfectly, can shut them down before they begin. For others, the future itself is frightening, and planning further ahead than the next half hour might bring up severe anxiety.

Finally, Time Transitions throw many NDs for a loop. Once they get into a task, switching to something else can feel almost impossible. It's as if their attention, once firmly focused on an activity, becomes stuck, as a magnet to steel. And not just any magnet, but a neodymium-iron-boron magnet that can hold up to 34 tons. How can a mere idea, like "I should go to bed," ever hope to overcome such a force? Try explaining to your partner that you literally cannot simply stop doing a thing and move on to something completely different. If your partner has never experienced this for themselves, it can be hard to relate, but it's worth taking the time to share your experience with Time Transitions.

Just because managing time can be difficult doesn't mean you can't conquer it. You just need to have strategies so you can be the master of your own time. Here are some Red Light/Green Light tips that might help.

RED LIGHT/GREEN LIGHT TIPS FOR TIME MANAGEMENT

 RED LIGHT: Time Comprehension Issues

 Green Lights:

- Do share with your partner that you do not have a natural understanding of the passage of time and that you struggle to predict how long something might take.
- Do be honest about your time confusion rather than randomly guessing when asked when you can be ready to go; your guess is likely to be incorrect and lead to lack of trust.

Chapter 7: Loving Time

- Do start thinking about time relatively to things with a set time. Think about whether a task takes about as long as watching a sitcom (usually thirty minutes) or a TV drama (around an hour) or a full-length movie (a couple of hours). This can help put time in perspective.
- Do train yourself to better understand time. Use a stopwatch or timing function on your phone to time things you do daily, such as taking a shower, getting dressed, or doing dishes. Record your times for a week and then figure the average. Keep a note to yourself of how long it usually takes you to do these tasks. Don't forget to factor in special considerations, such as whether you're getting ready to run out to the store, or getting ready for a fancy date, which might take longer. When you have a better handle on time in your daily life, your relationship won't get bogged down in petty arguments over being late. You have better things to do with your time. If using a timer is stressful to you because of ticking or an alarm, or just a history of negative experiences with timers, you don't need to use one. Instead, just write down what time you started a task and what time you finished it, then do the math to see how long it took.

Relating While Autistic

 Green Lights:

- Do make a commitment to plan out your time on a calendar or planning notebook or app to ensure that important things get done rather than forgotten. This includes eating, resting, and recreation, as well as work assignments and household chores. If you forget to eat, you might become cranky, and your beloved doesn't deserve to have a cranky partner, do they? Self-care is primarily for you, but a side benefit is that it's also good for your loved ones.

- Do stick to your plan. Winging it is rarely effective when it comes to time management.

- Do start with a list. Before your day begins in earnest, write down the things that need to be done that day. Then go prioritize it by numbering each item. Transfer them to your schedule or calendar in the order that you prioritized them. At the end of the day, if you had seventeen tasks and only completed nine of them, at least you have the satisfaction of knowing the nine most important things got done. The others can be moved to tomorrow's list. If you find yourself moving the same items over to the next day multiple times,

Chapter 7: Loving Time

re-evaluate: Should you give it a high priority number and get it over with? Or delegate it, or drop it from your list? You can be a better partner after work if you have a system. You can focus on spending your free time with your partner, not with your mind on the tasks that didn't get done.

- Do be gentle with yourself. If you dropped a ball, forgive yourself, pick it up, and put it back on your list for tomorrow. It's never helpful to beat yourself up. Wouldn't you forgive your loved one if they struggled? Of course you would, and you deserve the same grace.

 RED LIGHT: Time Transition Issues

 Green Lights:

- Do be honest about the things that are hardest for you to transition away from. This won't mean you have to give up the things you love, but it is important to know which time thieves are affecting your relationship with time and ultimately perhaps with your partner.
- Do own up to your problem with time rather than ignoring the issue or hoping it will get better on its own. That's not how it works. If you are one of those people

whose attention can become riveted to one thing at the cost of everything else, it will take work to learn how to make changes. But you can do it. When the change is important to you, not just to other people, your power to change is magnified.

- Do take responsibility for your difficulty with time transitions, rather than blaming your partner for being the "bad guy" who wants you to stop doing the things you love. You are the master of your own time.

- Do keep on enjoying the activities you love an need to relax, unwind, and recharge. Just decide how much time you need to spend on them, and use strategies to transition away from them after your necessary after-work down time. This will make sure you also have time for your relationship and other things you want in your life.

- Do use gradual transitions with intermediate steps. If you're engrossed in a video game or a deep-dive down a research rabbit hole, you shouldn't expect to immediately switch from a highly preferred and compelling activity to something that's not fun at all. Who could drop their favorite game and immediately start doing the dishes, just like that? Not many. Instead, give yourself mini-steps.

Chapter 7: Loving Time

Do plan to transition from your game or computer to something less intensely fascinating, something fairly neutral. Going from an online search to reading a chapter in a book is one suggestion. Walking around the block is another way to clear the mind. After you've read a chapter or walked around the block, or whatever your transition activity is, it will be easier to take on the chore you've set for yourself, such as washing dishes.

Do give yourself a break. Is the above still too difficult a step? Add other incremental baby steps, such as taking a tour around your house looking for stray glasses or dishes that got left around. Then take what you gathered to the kitchen, where you'll be in position for the ultimate task: washing the dishes. Be creative in finding transitional steps from your most desired activity to your least desired (but necessary) task. Your partner might help you come up with ideas. When figuring out a workable transition is difficult, facing it as a team can be easier than trying to tackle it alone.

Do reward yourself after you do the thing you didn't want to do. Is there something fun that you and your partner enjoy doing together? Schedule it for right after you finish your difficult job, and you'll have something to look forward to. Transitioning from a disliked task to an enjoyable one is the best kind of transition, and it makes it worth the work you put in.

WHAT SHALL WE TALK ABOUT?

Family Meeting Discussion Openers about Together Time

Ask and answer any or all of these questions, taking turns with your partner:

1. Is Time Comprehension a potential problem in your relationship? Have there been times that one or both of you felt at a loss as to how to predict how long something might take? Would any of the Green Light solutions for Time Comprehension be useful for you?

2. Is Time Planning difficult for you two? Does time just seem to happen to you, rather than the feeling that you can control or plan it? Have there been times that one or both of you wanted to plan something and get it on the calendar, or break it down into steps, but met resistance from your beloved? Could the Green Light solutions for Time Planning help?

3. Is Time Transitioning a possible roadblock in your relationship? Do either or both of you get so caught up in something that you

Chapter 7: Loving Time

find it nearly impossible to stop doing it and move on? Do you feel using the Green Light suggestions for Time Transitioning might be a good idea?

DATE NIGHT THEME

Keeper of the Time Share

Take turns sharing who gets to be the Keeper of Time for your next two date nights. The Keeper of Time gets to decide how the two of you will share your time together. Will it be dining out? Ordering in? Going to a movie? Binge-watching something old and comforting, or something new and exciting? Reading out loud to each other in front of the fireplace? Going bowling or skating or playing a board game? While the Keeper of Time gets to choose how your time will be spent on your date, remember to be merciful. Do not choose something your partner will find aversive, such as running a marathon when their speed is a stroll around the block. Choosing how you spend your time together is important, and it's something to be shared.

Relating While Autistic

FICTIONAL COUPLES

Trish & Bill

"Are you all right, sweetheart?"

Trish looked up from her computer to see Bill standing in his bathrobe, looking concerned.

"Of course, I'm fine, Bill. Why wouldn't I be?"

"Well, it's 3:00 AM, and you said you'd be coming right to bed five hours ago. I fell asleep waiting, and then when I woke up you weren't there. Have you been working all night?"

Trish blinked. "No. I mean, maybe." She squinted at the time on her screen. "Yes, I guess I have been. I'm sorry, I didn't notice the time. I was researching... stuff."

"Stuff, like work stuff?"

"Actually," Trish smiled sheepishly, "I've been reading about time management. Remember the other day when you had to work late and I said I'd have dinner ready, but I got involved on the computer and forgot?"

"I remember." Bill sat down beside her on the couch. "So, what are you learning?"

"Well, I think one of my problems with time management is transitions. I just can't seem to stop doing one thing and move on to something else. It's really, really hard for me, Bill. I've tried, but I keep getting sucked back down the rabbit hole."

Chapter 7: Loving Time

"It looks like it happened again tonight, didn't it?" Bill was smiling a little, so she knew he wasn't mad at her. He was such a gem!

"Well, yes. But at least I'm learning something to try next time. I need to plan out stepping-stone transition activities. It's like I'm on this side of a river with my computer, and the next thing I need to do is on the other side of the river. I can't jump across it; it's too wide."

"I get that." Bill nodded sleepily. "So, how do you get across?"

"I need stepping stones, like rocks in the river. If I can jump on the first rock, I'll be okay, and the computer will be behind me. But then I might need another rock to jump on to get all the way to the other side."

"I can picture it. But what are the rocks?"

"Well, if I need to transition from my computer to the kitchen, the first rock might be reading a page or two from one of my cookbooks."

"You mean those online recipe blogs? You've made some great dishes you got from them."

"True, I love my food blogs, but if I'm still on my phone or computer, that's not a good rock for me. I need to get up and get one of my cookbooks off the shelf. Turning paper pages is different from scrolling, but it's also satisfying and I enjoy it."

"Sounds good. What's your next rock?"

Relating While Autistic

"Let me think. Oh, I've got it. My next rock on the way to the kitchen will be to take a houseplant tour and check each one to see if it needs watering, and water the dry ones. Then, when I take the watering can back to the kitchen, I'll already be there, on the kitchen side of the river."

"You're brilliant. What about going to bed?"

"Well, my going-to-bed rocks could be reading a poem and doing my Crescent Moon yoga pose, and then going through my usual nighttime routine."

Bill yawned. "That's great, Trish, but I meant, what about going to bed, you and me, tonight?"

Trish giggled as she shut down her computer. "I'm right behind you. I won't need any rocks to help me get across that river tonight."

Justin & Maggie

"Justin, I'm tired of sleeping on this fold-out sofa bed."

"Yeah, it's really lumpy. Should we get a new one?"

"No, I don't want a new sofa bed. I want to sleep in our own room, on our own comfy bed."

"That'll be great. And it will be so calming with the new blue paint."

"I love the color. That's not the problem. The problem is you said you could finish painting the bedroom on one Saturday, and we've been sleeping on this sofa for over a month."

Chapter 7: Loving Time

"Has it really been that long?"

'You started the paint job on Fourth of July weekend, and now it's almost Labor Day. You do the math."

"Well, I could have done the painting itself in one day, but there was all that taping, and you made me get drop cloths—"

"I was not having you drip paint all over our furniture and carpet."

"Right, right, it was a good idea. But that meant I had to go to the hardware store for drop cloths. And back again for different sized brushes and rollers."

"And again for a ladder, and more paint when you ran out."

"Right. So that added on to the time it took to paint."

"Well, the painting itself took a lot longer than one day once you got started. You said it was a Saturday job."

Justin sighed. "I was way off on that. I had no idea how long that was going to take. It's just four walls, but it needed two coats. Who knew? But at least it's finally finished."

"Is it, though?" Maggie raised an eyebrow.

"Sure, all four walls, two coats, a beautiful blue."

"Then why aren't we sleeping in our own bed?"

"Well, all that's left is details."

"Details like taking down the tape, putting away the drop cloths, extra paint, paint brushes and rollers, and the ladder? Putting the furniture back where it belongs? Those details?"

"Yeah, that's all that's left."

Relating While Autistic

"Well, it's been all that's left for a week now. When were you planning to actually take care of those details?"

"I guess that's the problem, I didn't plan for them. Mentally I moved on once the painting was finished." Justin gave Maggie a sidelong look. "I don't suppose you'd want to take care of the details for me, would you? Now that I've done the hard part?"

"Oh, no. You were the one who wanted a blue bedroom, I was the one who said it would be too much work and I didn't want to do it. But I agreed after you promised you'd do the whole thing by yourself, on one Saturday. So no, don't look to me to clean up your mess."

"You're right, I will do it. It's not such a big job. I could probably do it in, like, ten minutes."

"Show me."

"What do you mean?"

"Set your timer for ten minutes, and go for it. I'll make iced coffee for you when you're done."

Justin set his timer and got to work. When it rang after ten minutes, he still had a lot to do, but Maggie said she would put the iced coffee in the fridge and get out some cookies to go with it. After an hour, Justin came out, tired but proud of himself.

"You should see how great our bedroom looks now!" he said.

Maggie agreed. In fact, it looked so lovely and inviting that they decided to let the iced coffee and cookies wait while they enjoyed their new blue room.

Chapter 7: Loving Time

Understanding how long a task would take, planning enough time to do it properly, and remembering that cleaning up afterwards is part of the job were helpful things for Justin to realize.

Lucia & Naima

"So, when shall we have our brunch date?" Lucia scrolled through her phone calendar.

"Oh, I don't know. Whenever you want," said Naima. "Any time is fine with me."

"Great! This Sunday, then."

"Wait, I might have a thing with my mom this Sunday."

"You might, or you do? We can make it the next Sunday."

"Sure. Unless that's the Sunday I have the thing."

"Well, what is 'the thing,' and which Sunday is it?"

"It's one of those mother-daughter teas at her church. I promised to go with her."

"No problem, we'll make ours on another Sunday. So, which Sunday is it? Can you check your emails or texts from her and see?"

"Hmm...I'm not sure. Mom was talking to me on speaker phone while I was driving, so I couldn't write down the date. I figured I'd remember it anyway. I know it was on a Sunday."

"What about a Saturday for our brunch, then? Maybe this Saturday?"

Relating While Autistic

"Yeah, maybe, if I don't have to help my little sister clean out her closets. That was supposed to be one of these Saturdays."

Lucia put down her phone. "Naima, how are we supposed to make plans to spend time together if you don't know when you're free?"

"I know, I'm terrible with organization. It always seems like I'll remember the dates because at that moment, it's the most important thing. Then the rest of life happens and all the dates get jumbled up in my memory."

"You need a system," suggested Lucia.

"That's for sure. Should I go buy one of those calendar-journal books?"

"Well, you could. But would you always have it with you?"

"Probably not."

"Why don't you use your phone calendar, like I do?"

"I never even opened that app on my new phone. It seems complicated. I don't need one more thing to figure out."

"This is a tool that will help you remember all the things. You can even use voice activation to set appointments and reminders, hands free."

"It would be a huge relief not to try to remember everything and worry that I'm dropping something out."

"I can help you set it up. Once you get started, it'll be easy, you'll see."

Chapter 7: Loving Time

"Okay, let's do it. Because I definitely want to get our brunch date on the calendar as soon as possible! Just as long as it doesn't conflict with the mom thing."

"Naima, is it possible the mom thing is on Mother's Day?"

"Maybe. Is that a specific day?"

"Every year. Don't worry, I'll help you put it on your phone."

Naima needed a system to help her plan and remember important events so she could be in control of her time.

Daisy & Crow

Daisy and Crow are at Daisy's apartment, putting together a jigsaw puzzle while listening to music. Daisy likes turning the pieces upside down so she won't be distracted by the colors, and Crow is happy to stick to the straight edges and let her do the middle.

DAISY: So, when are we going to move in together?

CROW: Oh, sometime. It makes sense. It'll save money, and we spend most of our time together anyway. Why pay double rent?

DAISY: I already know why we decided to live together. I'm asking when.

CROW: Well, I don't know. Whenever we're ready, I guess.

DAISY: I'm ready now. When will you be ready?

CROW: I can't put my feelings on a timeline. I guess I'll know when I'm ready, when I'm ready.

Relating While Autistic

DAISY: So, you'll know you're ready, when you're ready to know when you'll know you're ready, is that what you're saying?

CROW: I just don't like to think about the future. I like living in the here and now. The future stresses me out. Anything could happen. Look at the state the world is in.

DAISY: The world could be in the same state, but we'd be living together instead of separately. That seems better to me. I thought you felt the same way. Are you afraid we'll break up and have to find different places to live?

CROW: No, I trust you. I trust us. We're definitely not going to break up. I just don't trust the rest of the world.

DAISY: Well, imhbeo, it's none of the rest of the world's business.

CROW: imh—what?

DAISY: In my humble but educated opinion. Imhbeo.

CROW: That's not a thing.

DAISY: It's a thing now. I just made it a thing. I spoke it into existence. Just like we spoke living together into existence when we decided to live together. It's real. We just have to catch up to the realness.

CROW: How do we "catch up to the realness?"

DAISY: It's easy. You give your landlord notice, start packing your stuff, and move in here. Then we split expenses instead of paying for everything twice. We could save up and buy a car, no more public transportation.

Chapter 7: Loving Time

CROW: And you think we should do this now.

DAISY: We'd be fools not to.

CROW: Daisy, I want to wake up every morning next to you, and I want to hear your adorable snore as I fall asleep every night.

DAISY: I don't snore, but do go on.

CROW: Disagree. Unimportant. The truth is, I do want to live with you. Thinking about the future and taking the steps to make it happen, though, that's hard for me. But I trust you. If you hold on to me and drag me through this, I know we'll get to the other side together.

DAISY: I would drag you through hell, through broken glass, through shag carpet on our knees, to be together.

CROW: Let's hope it doesn't come to that. Shag leaves the worst carpet burns.

For Crow, making a decision was one thing, but thinking about the future, and then actually making a timeline and following through on the decision, was another thing entirely. They were glad Daisy was willing to stand by them in spite of their procrastination and pull them through.

Relating While Autistic

THEY SAY

We really don't have an issue with time. She has a space where she can go and play Sims in our extra room in the house, and I can play with my friend Rocket League on PlayStation in the living room. We do a lot of things together as a family with our daughter, Claire, but when Claire goes to bed, some days we like our separate time.

— Thomas McDonald III

This one, time, is tricky. I love my partner, and I also need time alone to recharge. Although I miss him when he goes on trips, I use that time to completely shut down and do the absolute minimum. I like the house completely quiet if I am reading a book, or I play goofy music if I am in a mood to clean or do a project. I sing and dance around the house like Fred Astaire with my mop and broom. It's fun and I am free to be silly! If I am recovering from a difficult episode, sometimes it's better for everyone to just leave me alone for a while. I'm okay! I'm just recovering. He understands, acknowledges my needs, and is respectful. We are always so happy to see each other when he comes home!

— Wendy B.

Chapter 7: Loving Time

We decided to carve out time specifically for the two of us to do something we enjoy and get some more breathing space. Maybe that's reading books in a coffee shop, going for a spa afternoon, or getting drinks at our favorite hometown haunt. We also made it clear to our families that they have to ask us first before booking up our time.

— Tara, autistic woman, married to a man with ADHD

Chapter 8

Loving Works

"A thousand words will not leave so deep an impression as one deed."

— Henrik Ibsen

Chapter 8: Loving Works

L oving Works means doing things for your loved one to demonstrate how you feel, rather than simply saying the words "I love you." It relates to one of Gary Chapman's 5 Love Languages: Acts of Service. Chapman says this means "doing things your [partner] would like you to do. They require thought, planning, time, effort, and energy. If done with a positive spirit, they are indeed expressions of love."

If Loving Works is your partner's primary expressive love language, you may notice that they do things for you, such as chores and fixing things around the house, more often than they send you flowers or write you love letters. Doing these things is their way of saying, "I love you." If you've been waiting for verbal declarations, you may have been missing the nonverbal love letters they've been sending all along.

If your partner's primary receptive love language is Loving Works, it may not matter to them how often you draw hearts in the steam of the bathroom mirror. They'd much rather you pick up the used towels, launder them, and put them away. Doing things to keep your household running smoothly is an important way to send the message that you value and cherish your beloved.

In Amythest Schaber's description of one ND love language, Support Swapping, partners take turns doing things for one another, especially when either partner is at a low ebb or is out of "spoons."

Relating While Autistic

Are you familiar with the "Spoon Theory?" It was created by Christine Miserandino on her blog, "But You Don't Look Sick." It helps explain the concept of the toll that invisible disabilities can take, using a metaphor of spoons as units of physical or mental energy. Neuromajority people usually have a nearly unlimited amount of "spoons" to get them through the things they need and want to do on any given day. However, if you're a "spoonie," someone with a condition such as lupus, fibromyalgia, or chronic fatigue, you don't get many spoons, and you can't easily regenerate new spoons. If you spent all your spoons for the morning taking a shower and fixing yourself breakfast, you won't have enough spoons to do laundry or dishes.

Many autistic folk can relate to this. For them, social and sensory experiences can deplete their spoons rapidly, so they have none left for self-regulation or self-care. They might need long periods of quiet alone time while they wait for spoon regeneration to be able to get back to the business of life.

With Support Swapping, when one partner notices the other is about out of spoons, they step up and lend a hand. That might mean putting your partner's dishes in the sink for them or laying out their medications. It might mean bringing your loved one a bottle of water or fixing them a sandwich when you notice they may have too few spoons to take care of themselves.

Chapter 8: Loving Works

Support Swapping is a two-way street, of course, as is Chapman's Acts of Service love language. If doing things for a loved one always goes in only one direction, it can lead to one partner feeling used. Even a spoonie with a lot of needs can find ways of showing their beloved that they love doing things for them. One might have the mental spoons to plan menus for the week but no energy left to cook. Their partner might have the physical spoons to prepare the meals but would get bogged down trying to decide what to cook. Support Swapping lets each partner show their support through Loving Works that are within their capabilities.

 RED LIGHT/GREEN LIGHT TIPS FOR LOVING WORKS

 RED LIGHT: **You keep doing nice things for your partner, but they don't seem to notice or care.**

 Green Lights:

- Do let them know that you love them. If their receptive love language is different, they may not recognize your Loving Works as a demonstration of your love.
- Do keep on doing nice things for your partner, unless they tell you they don't want you to do those things

for them. If you feel loving when you do things for them, even if it's not their receptive language, you can continue. Just be sure that those are the things they really want done. For example, if you surprise them by doing their laundry without asking, you might find that they have special ways of laundering certain items, and your Loving Work might backfire.

- Do remember the "Golden Rule" and do for them what they would like, rather than what you assume they would like. Ask.

 RED LIGHT: You feel like Cinderella doing all the work and your partner isn't helping.

 Green Lights:

- Do let your partner know how you feel. Discuss fair ways of dividing chores in a way that makes sense for you two.
- Do resist the temptation to go on a "work strike" to show your partner how much work you've been doing by quitting. This never ends happily, and there's a lot more work to do at the end of it. If you feel unappreciated, don't strike, talk. Bring it up during a Family Meeting and share your feelings.

Chapter 8: Loving Works

- Do discuss your love languages, your "spoon" status, and the need to support swap at times.

RED LIGHT: Your partner keeps doing things around the house, and you feel guilty that you're not doing as much as they are.

Green Lights:

- Do schedule a family meeting to talk about how you divide up family chores. Make a plan that feels fair to you both, keeping in mind each partner's strengths and preferences.
- Do let your partner know that you appreciate what they do, and that you feel guilty for not doing more yourself. Find out if they're feeling resentful or if they truly enjoy doing the things they're doing for the household.
- Do break free from traditional gender roles. Yard work is not "men's work" and kitchen work is not "women's work." If she loves to garden and he loves to cook, that's what they should do, regardless of how their parents divided up household chores in the past.

Relating While Autistic

WHAT SHALL WE TALK ABOUT?

Family Meeting Discussion Openers about Loving Works

Ask and answer any or all of these questions, taking turns with your partner:

1. How do you feel about the way we handle chores as a couple? Does it seem equitable, each of us doing what we can for the household, whether or not it's exactly equal?
2. What changes could we make to ensure no one feels overburdened or underappreciated?
3. Each of you asks your beloved: Is there something I can do for you that would make your life easier or happier this week?

DATE NIGHT THEME

Share the Load

Date Night doesn't have to be fancy or expensive, as long as you two are together, enjoying one another's company. A trip to the grocery store or laundromat, just the two of you with no kids along for the ride, could become a date if you play it right. What would make these chores into Date Night expressions of Loving Works?

Chapter 8: Loving Works

Dancing together while your laundry is spinning dry? Sneaking a kiss if you find yourselves alone in the frozen foods aisle? As long it's fun for both of you, there's no reason why chores can't also be expressions of love. After the laundry and groceries are put away, the two of you can relax with a cup of tea, a glass of wine, a romantic movie, or whatever makes it feel like a date.

FICTIONAL COUPLES

Trish & Bill

Bill hovered in the kitchen doorway watching while Trish prepared dinner.

"Isn't there anything I can do to help?" he asked again.

"No, thank you, I've got it covered." Trish smiled at him over her shoulder before returning to her work, and he noticed how adorable she looked with a smudge of flour on her nose.

"Maybe I could..." He trailed off. What could he do? He knew nothing about cooking. His mother had ruled the kitchen his whole life, and he and his father were not allowed to even cross the threshold while she worked her mysterious magic.

She stopped, put down her spoon, and turned to him. "What is it?" she asked. "Don't you want to read or watch TV?"

"I'd rather be with you. It looks like you're working too hard, and I'm no help at all."

Relating While Autistic

Trish came over and gave him a kiss. "This isn't hard work for me, I love cooking. I love our arrangement where I cook and you clean up. It seems like I got the best part, though. Did you want to trade?"

"No, no, I'm happy to do the dishes after you've done all the cooking. It just seems to me that I have the easy part and you have the heaviest load. I want to help, but I don't know how." He sighed "I'm useless in the kitchen."

Trish hugged him. "You're not useless at all! I hate doing the dishes, the sound of the plates against each other is horrible for me! And I really do enjoy cooking."

"It looks like you're having fun in here."

"Do you want to join the fun?" Trish asked. "Maybe it's too lonely in the living room right now."

"I'm usually lonely when I'm not with you. I used to love being alone, and I still do sometimes, but being near you always feels right to me. Like everything is going to be okay."

"Well, okay, then. Put on an apron, wash your hands, and I'll teach you how to be my sous chef."

For Trish and Bill, sharing meal duties by having Trish cook and Bill clean up had been a good idea. It was traditional, but it also suited their preferences. Changing it up by teaching Bill to help out in the kitchen gave them more enjoyable together time and helped Bill feel like he was making a more meaningful contribution.

Chapter 8: Loving Works

Justin & Maggie

Maggie scrubbed the burnt cheese on the bottom of the casserole dish. It had been a long day. She was more than ready to sit down, put her feet up, and finally relax. She wanted to let the worries of the day retreat into the background of a sitcom laugh track, but this pan wasn't going to scrub itself.

"Hey, Maggie," she heard Justin call. "Don't worry about the kitchen stuff, come on in here. You've had a rough day. You should just relax." It was a pleasant surprise to have Justin offer to do the kitchen cleanup for once.

"Thank you, Justin!" She sank into the couch cushions and let him tuck her in with an afghan on her lap and a pillow behind her. "This was just what I needed!"

As soon as she was settled in, Justin sat back down beside her.

"What are you doing?" she asked.

"Watching TV with you, of course. Why?"

"I thought you were going to do the dishes."

Justin looked surprised. "Why did you think that?"

"Well, you told me I didn't have to worry about them."

"Oh, I just meant you could do them later. They're not going anywhere."

Maggie picked up the remote, turned off the TV, and just looked at him.

"I'm sensing something," he said. "You're not happy."

Relating While Autistic

"You think?" She raised an eyebrow.

"You're not happy because … you don't want to do the dishes later?"

"I never want to do the dishes. I hate it. I only do it because you hate the sound the silverware makes when it jangles together, and I love you. But the silverware is already taken care of, and I don't love scrubbing pots and pans."

"You don't?"

"I hate it, actually, but I was in the middle of doing it. When you called me in here, I assumed you were offering to do it for me because I had such a bad day. But my bad day will not be any better if I have to go back into that kitchen later and see the same dirty pot in the sink."

"So, I'm guessing, you want me to do it?"

"I do."

"Maybe after the show?" She kept looking at him, and not turning the TV back on. "Or, maybe right now?"

"Good idea." After he stood up and started towards the kitchen, she pointed the remote toward the TV.

"But you're not going to watch our next episode without me, are you?"

"I would never do that," she said, finding a rerun to watch instead. "And, Justin?"

"Yes?"

Chapter 8: Loving Works

"Thank you. Really. I hated that job, and it means a lot to me that you're doing it."

"Even though you had to spell it out for me?"

"Yes. I really appreciate it, and it makes me feel loved and cared for."

Justin took on the scrubbing task with a bit of a smile, knowing that this was another way he could show Maggie how much he loved her. He was grateful that she understood how he felt about the sound of the silverware, but that shouldn't mean she had to do all the dirty work in the kitchen. Next time he'd offer to scrub the pots and pans before she had to ask him to do it.

Lucia & Naima

"Naima? Come on down," Lucia called. "I've made your breakfast." Lucia put the finishing touches on the table.

"You what?" Naima stood in the doorway.

"I made your breakfast. Scrambled eggs with cheese and toast points, juice, coffee. It's all on the table for you." Lucia smiled expectantly, while Naima just stood and stared.

"I usually make my own breakfast," she said, still by the door.

"But today, you don't have to. Think of it as a little 'I love you' note in the form of food. Come on, sit down, let's eat!"

Naima sat and stared at her plate. "I usually just have toast and coffee," she said.

Relating While Autistic

"But today you get a treat, a full, cooked breakfast."

"The toast is cut in triangles instead of rectangles."

"I know, right? Triangles are so much better." Lucia started eating, and then noticed that Naima hadn't picked up her fork. "What's wrong, don't you like it?"

Naima took a deep breath and said nothing at first. Finally she said, "Lucia, I love that you did all this for me. I love you for taking care of me. It is incredibly sweet and thoughtful of you."

"I sense a 'but' coming." Lucia put her fork down.

"But I can't eat this. The eggs are squishy, the toast is the wrong shape, and the juice will make my teeth hurt. I have a breakfast routine, always the same."

"I know, but I wanted to surprise you with a treat. A special breakfast."

"Surprises are not a treat for me. I just want to have my toast rectangles and drink my coffee in the morning, not eat all this. And before you go and try to fix it for me, the preparation is part of my routine. I do it the same way every morning because I like doing it."

"Oh, I get it. Your breakfast routine is like my tooth-brushing routine. It has to be the same for you every time, doesn't it?"

"Yes, it really does. I'm so sorry I can't appreciate this breakfast after you worked so hard on it."

Chapter 8: Loving Works

"Don't worry, just let me get this plate and glass off the table so you'll have room to do your usual breakfast routine." Lucia understood that if someone had a special routine, then changing it could throw off the whole day. She hadn't realized breakfast was a ritual for her partner, but she did understand the importance of personal rituals. She whisked the breakfast away out of Naima's sight, and Naima went to make her own toast and coffee.

Lucia learned that doing something for your partner to show your love is only loving if they actually want it done. Honoring your beloved's wishes is a sign of respect.

Daisy & Crow

Daisy and Crow unpack boxes after moving in together.

CROW: Here, let me get that for you. (*They take the box Daisy was carrying and put it on the floor.*)

DAISY: Thanks. (*She brings in another box, and Crow puts down the box they were carrying to take the one Daisy has.*)

CROW: I've got it.

DAISY: I guess you do. I'll just start unpacking. (*She stoops to pick up a box from the floor to put it on the table, but Crow does it for her. She picks up a knife to cut through the packing tape.*)

CROW: Whoa! Let me do that! (*They reach to take the knife from Daisy, but she holds it away at arm's length.*)

Relating While Autistic

DAISY: Are you seriously afraid to let me use a knife? You do know I'm a full-grown adult and I know where you sleep.

CROW: (*Looking surprised*) I'm not afraid. I'm just helping you.

DAISY: You're infantilizing me, is what you're doing.

CROW: What? No. That's weird.

DAISY: You're the one making it weird, helicopter.

CROW: Are you too proud to let someone else help you?

DAISY: I will let you help me all day long when I need help, but all this hovering and taking things I'm trying to do is not helpful. It feels like you don't trust me, like you think I'm a child.

CROW: I definitely do not think of you as a child, weirdo. That's just gross.

DAISY: Then back off. I've got this.

CROW: Since you asked so nicely, and you're still holding the knife, I am backing off now. This is me, backing off. (*Crow holds up their hands and steps away from her.*)

DAISY: Thank you. Why don't you get the rest of the boxes inside while I start putting things away? (*She cuts through the packing tape and opens the box, taking out several mason jars filled with dry beans. Crow comes in with more boxes.*) Hey, Crow, what are these for?

CROW: That's food. It's for when we want beans, but not canned beans.

Chapter 8: Loving Works

DAISY: Oh, yes, of course. I, too, would prefer to soak beans overnight and cook them all day long rather than using a can opener. These are going to the back of the top shelf.

CROW: Let me do that— (*They stop when they see the look on Daisy's face.*) Or not. I just meant, I am tall enough to reach the top shelf, and you, well...

DAISY: I realize that I am vertically challenged...

CROW: Fun-sized?

DAISY: But my step ladder grants me plus 20 in height and reach.

CROW: Oh, I didn't know you had a step ladder.

DAISY: (*Taking it from beside the refrigerator and unfolding it*) I love my step ladder. I never knew my real ladder.

CROW: (*Chuckles in spite of themself*) Remind me to never get between a weirdo and her step ladder. Do you want me to hold it for you?

DAISY: (*glares*)

CROW: I'll take that as a 'No' and let you get on with it. By yourself. Because you don't need me.

DAISY: It's not that I don't need you, I just don't need you doing things for me that I can do for myself.

CROW: I guess we still have a lot to learn about each other, huh?

DAISY: Which will be easier now that we're living together. But I know something you can do for me that would really help.

CROW: Name it.

Relating While Autistic

DAISY: Can you hang those pictures on the wall over there?

CROW: Sure, easy.

DAISY: Easy for you maybe, not me. I always worry I'm going to hammer a nail into an electrical wire and electrocute myself.

CROW: You know you can figure out where the studs are, right?

DAISY: No, you can figure out where the studs are. I'm not risking my life.

CROW: Aren't you afraid I'll get electrocuted?

DAISY: You're strong, you'll probably survive.

CROW: Never fear, I will hang all of the pictures. That means I get to decide what goes where.

DAISY: Fine with me. I hate hanging stuff on walls more than I hate coming across a gelatinous cube in D&D. I can't stand those wibbly-wobbly jerks!

CROW: Note to self: Never make Jell-O for Daisy.

THEY SAY

"Loving Works" is still a work in progress for us. Our house is mostly geared towards my needs specifically. I have to prepare the food because if one thing is wrong, I won't eat it. I need to have certain types of socks, shirts, pants. My specific things can't be moved

Chapter 8: Loving Works

without me knowing or there's some issues. We need to talk about moving furniture around because it will have a two-week effect on me. I do try and reciprocate, listening to what she needs.

— Thomas McDonald III

Oh gosh, safe to say when it comes to "Loving Works" I am usually the one who needs taking care of! Even so, I want to do my part. I do nice things around the house for him, and he is good enough to notice! The toilet paper is always replaced. The plants are watered. I like doing laundry, so I carefully fold and put it away. He always has a clean towel. I like cooking and baking healthy foods and I put a lot of thought into my menus. I fix him a sliced apple to take to work and I draw cute pictures on the plastic container for him, or write I LOVE YOU on a napkin and put it in his lunch. I never had a mommy, but I wanted one. The things I did for my children when they were little, the Mommy things, I do for him. And he notices. That's the beauty part. He likes that I dote on him, and he voices his appreciation. What I do matters!

— Wendy B.

PART III

LISTEN! HEED THE WARNINGS & DON'T GET DERAILED!

"No long-term marriage is made easily...somehow or other, through grace, our failures can be redeemed and blessed."

— Madeleine L'Engle

"Howl said, 'I think we ought to live happily ever after,' and she thought he meant it. Sophie knew that living happily ever after with Howl would be a good deal more eventful than any story made it sound, though she was determined to try. 'It should be hair-raising,' added Howl."

— Diana Wynne Jones, *Howl's Moving Castle*

Chapter 9

Big 3 Hot Topics: Families, Money, and Sex

"By the time I met my husband I was pretty well convinced I would never understand anyone well enough to maintain something everlasting... From the moment I met Tom, I sensed he was a great deal like me... Like bookends, we have learned to support each other when the small stuff in the middle pushes us apart."

— Liane Holliday Willey, *Pretending to be Normal*

Chapter 9: Big 3 Hot Topics: Families, Money, and Sex

Issues that can get in the way of a relationship running smoothly include disagreements stemming from three hot topics: families, money, and sex. Couples everywhere deal with these same potential roadblocks, and how you manage these hot topics says a lot about the strength of your relationship.

As with all issues, it is never on one partner alone to make changes or compromise. Strong relationships allow for each of you to both support and be supported as needed, much like the bookends Liane Holliday Willey described in the quote above.

Family problems may be related to child-rearing or to relationships with in-laws and extended families. Before entering into a long-term relationship or marriage, it's important to discuss whether or not you want to have children and talk about your parenting styles. You don't want to wait until you have a child to realize that you have major differences in your parenting beliefs. For example, one of you might believe that babies should be picked up when they cry so they can learn that the world is a safe place where they will be cared for, while the other parent may believe babies should be left alone to cry it out so they can learn to self-soothe. Start the conversations long before your first pregnancy, so that by the time you welcome your new arrival, you'll be ready to co-parent as a team.

Many couples find that coming from different types of families of origin can cause strain, especially if the in-laws have conflicting views. Too many newlyweds find themselves eating two Thanksgiving dinners rather than turning down either parents' invitation. Make sure the two of you are united, having discussed what's best for you as a couple before talking to your parents about your choices. Open communication and setting boundaries and expectations will go a long way.

Money is another thing many couples fight over. How did your parents handle budgeting and bill-paying in your childhood? If money was scarce for you, you might find yourself pinching every penny to save for the rainy day you believe is inevitable. Or you might spend extravagantly to make up for your years of thrift. One partner might have a shopping addiction which should be dealt with.

Before you move in together and start sharing expenses, have a serious planning discussion about how the two of you will handle money. Make a budget to avoid anxiety about being able to pay the bills. Make a plan for surplus money after the bills are paid so you can save for your future retirement and put something away for unexpected repairs. Start a savings account for your taxes so you don't have to dread April 15th. Make sure each of you has some money budgeted that you can spend on whatever makes you happy, whether it's fancy coffee, new shoes, or your own savings account. Knowing how much money you have coming in and going out is important to let you feel secure rather than worried about money.

Chapter 9: Big 3 Hot Topics: Families, Money, and Sex

Sex is another thing many couples disagree about. How often is often enough? Who should initiate? This is an area where partners' self-esteem can take a big hit, and it can be difficult to talk about intimate things. It's important to clear the air and be upfront about how you feel about your love life. If one partner is in the mood and the other isn't, what's the best way to say "No" without anyone feeling personally rejected? Talking about these issues in advance, when you're outside the bedroom, is important.

When it comes to these three hot topics, stay focused on what's important—your love for one another—and you can keep your relationship from going off the tracks.

 ## RED LIGHT/GREEN LIGHT TIPS FOR FAMILY ISSUES

 RED LIGHT: Even though you're both usually on the same page and discuss parenting philosophy, sometimes it comes down to a decision that must be made in the moment and you don't have time to consult each other. How do you make the call?

 Green Lights:

- Do commit to respecting your co-parent and making sure your children know how you feel.

- Do resist the urge to undermine your co-parent. If they made a call, even if you don't necessarily agree with it, wait until you're alone to talk about it. Your kids should see a united front.

- Do take a moment before making a decision when a new situation arises and you haven't discussed it with your partner yet. There's no need to rush to a final decision, even if your sweet child is asking you, "Pretty please?" with those puppy dog eyes. Don't jump to a "Yes" if there's any chance their other parent might not agree.

- Do consider having areas of expertise assigned. For example, one parent takes the lead on educational decisions, and the other on health decisions, if you have knowledge and experience in these fields.

 ## RED LIGHT/GREEN LIGHT TIPS FOR MONEY ISSUES

RED LIGHT: One or both of you came to the relationship with significant debt, such as student loans, medical bills, credit card debt, or a gambling or shopping addiction.

Chapter 9: Big 3 Hot Topics: Families, Money, and Sex

Green Lights:

- Do put all of your cards on the table. Don't hold back on your financial picture. It can be embarrassing to admit that you went crazy with your first credit cards and now you're drowning in a debt that keeps getting bigger and bigger as you pay the minimum payment each month. But, no matter how much you want to put your best foot forward and minimize the negative parts of your life, you need to tell the truth.

- Do listen to your partner's financial sharing without giving them any shame or blame. If your partner tells you about a big debt you didn't know about, thank them for their honesty. It won't help to make them feel even worse about it than they already do. It's not easy to admit when we're in trouble, and telling you the truth about their debt is an important way of saying that they love and trust you.

- Do get professional help from a respected consumer credit agency. There's no shame in seeking out the support you need, and you are not alone in this.

Relating While Autistic

 ## RED LIGHT/GREEN LIGHT TIPS FOR INTIMACY ISSUES

 RED LIGHT: You experience chronic fatigue, and sex is sometimes painful or exhausting for you, but you love your partner and want to make them happy.

 Green Lights:

- Do talk to your doctor about painful intercourse and chronic fatigue. You deserve help and your doctor should listen and respect you.

- Do be honest with your partner. It's not helpful to keep quiet and "suffer" through sex rather than talking about your feelings. Don't let embarrassment or fear of hurting their feelings stop you from telling them the truth. Starting with honesty the way to a solution.

- Do tell them the truth. The first truth may be that you love your partner and find them sexy. The second truth may be that sometimes you're too exhausted or in too much pain to enjoy sex. This is not a reflection on their attractiveness or ability to please you, it's just a fact of your life.

- Do plan for times to be intimate when you're feeling your best. This might be in the middle of the day rather

Chapter 9: Big 3 Hot Topics: Families, Money, and Sex

than early morning or at bedtime. The important thing is for you both to be able to enjoy intimacy.

WHAT SHALL WE TALK ABOUT?

Family Meeting Discussion Openers about Hot Topics

Ask and answer any or all of these questions, taking turns with your partner:

1. What do each of you love and appreciate about your partner's parents and siblings? When have you had the most fun with extended family? What can you plan for the future to help maintain positive relationships with them in ways that work for the two of you?

2. Imagine you had a sudden windfall, such as winning the lottery or getting an unexpected tax refund. How would you want to spend it? After sharing all of your over-the-top ideas, such as retiring and traveling around the world, focus on the more accessible dreams, such as a weekend at the beach or a new dishwasher. Now, how can you two plan to save for that dream and make it happen?

3. What do you love most about your beloved's body? What about your own body? What's your favorite sexual position or something new you want to try? Make sure that both of you are on the same page and comfortable with new things.

DATE NIGHT THEME

Off-Limit Topics

Before your next Date Night, agree on a list of topics to avoid, such as children, in-laws, money, sex, and politics. Then enjoy focusing on one another rather than on the rest of the world.

FICTIONAL COUPLES

Trish & Bill

The holidays were coming, and Trish dreaded the thought. She knew her parents would want to see them for every single family tradition she'd grown up with. They would be lighting Advent candles every Sunday, caroling around the neighborhood, followed by cocoa with peppermint marshmallows, the first big shopping expedition with lunch at the mall, and the extended

Chapter 9: Big 3 Hot Topics: Families, Money, and Sex

family Christmas cookie exchange. Of course, everyone would go to watch her nieces and nephews sit on Santa's lap for photos, and then there was the Midnight candlelight service Christmas Eve, Christmas morning with stockings, Christmas brunch, and the formal Christmas dinner. They even had Boxing Day on the 26th when they gathered to eat leftovers and put together boxes of things to donate to charity. It was just too much!

Trish used to enjoy all of these family events when she was single. If she started to get overwhelmed, she could just go to her room and regulate in private and no one was bothered.

But now she had Bill to think of. Bill hated crowds. He hardly knew her family, so he hadn't had a chance to get comfortable with them. How could she ask him to devote so much of the month of December to her family? And what about his own family traditions? He'd never talked about them. Trish decided they needed to have a family meeting in early November to make a plan to survive December.

At the meeting, when she laid out for him all of the things her family usually did together during the Christmas season, he was silent and pale.

"So, what do you think about all this?" she asked.

"Think?" He took a deep breath and exhaled slowly. "Honestly, I don't know what to think. I had no idea people did all these things."

Relating While Autistic

"What does your family do?"

"We open one present on Christmas Eve, and stockings and gifts on Christmas morning, and have dinner, and that's it."

"That's pretty different from my family, isn't it?"

"Really different. So, will we have to do all those things? And what about my family, can we see them, too?"

"Of course we can see your family! They're your family, and I love them, too."

"Send in the clones?"

Trish laughed. "The technology isn't there yet."

"You know I want to make you and your family happy. I don't want them to think I took you away from them. But I just don't think I can do it all. I'm sorry, I wish I could."

He looked so sad Trish threw her arms around him and gave him a tight hug. "You don't have to do it all! Really! It's way too much."

"But they're your family."

"You're my family now. They're my relatives. We can make this work, I know we can. They shouldn't expect us to do everything with them the way I used to do when I was single."

"Okay, let's figure it out."

"Especially because, once we have children of our own, they'll need to respect our family boundaries."

"Children ... are you saying ... do you mean ... Are you ... ?"

Chapter 9: Big 3 Hot Topics: Families, Money, and Sex

"No, I'm not pregnant. You will be the first to know." Trish smiled and leaned her forehead against Bill's. "But someday, we will have children, and we will be the ones making decisions about our own family traditions, not the grandparents."

"You're right. I adore you. Let's figure this out."

For the rest of their family meeting, they made notes of which holiday events were most important to them, which they could do without, and what new traditions they wanted to establish for themselves as a new family. Although their parents would have liked to see more of them, they respected that Trish and Bill had to make their own decisions and protect themselves from social and sensory overload. Because they planned in advance not to get derailed by others' expectations, it turned out to be a wonderful first holiday for the newlyweds.

Justin & Maggie

"Is everything packed for the picnic? Are my deviled eggs in the cooler?" Justin repetitively tossed a small ball and caught it with one hand.

"You know I wouldn't forget to pack your famous deviled eggs. Your family wouldn't forgive us if we showed up without them."

"Well, I do make the best deviled eggs in the state."

"We've all heard about your blue ribbon from the state fair. Multiple times." Maggie added ice and closed the cooler chest. "It's not your deviled eggs I'm worried about, it's mine."

Relating While Autistic

Justin stopped tossing the ball and looked at her. "You didn't make any deviled eggs. I always make the deviled eggs."

"Not deviled eggs, my eggs."

"Your eggs? What are we talking about?"

"We're talking about how your family, and especially your mom, is always making cracks about my eggs. They want to know when we're getting pregnant, what are we waiting for, telling me I should freeze my eggs before it's too late. That whole thing."

"You can't freeze eggs in the shell, they'd probably explode. Who's telling you to freeze eggs?"

"Your mother wants me to freeze my personal eggs so we can use them later to get pregnant."

"Huh. I haven't heard that. Are you sure that's what she was talking about?"

"Yes, I'm sure. You don't hear her because every family picnic you're always with the guys, playing ball. You have no idea what I put up with."

"I thought you liked my family. You're 'putting up' with them?"

"Justin, I love your family. I do not love having their nose in my business, asking personal questions about when we're having a baby."

"Didn't you tell them we want some time to just be a couple before we start a family? Just tell them."

"I've told them a million times."

Chapter 9: Big 3 Hot Topics: Families, Money, and Sex

"I doubt—"

"Don't get all literal on me. I'm asking for your help."

"Okay, now you're talking. Tell me what you want, I've got your back."

"Thank you. Here's the plan: when we get to the picnic, don't rush off with your brothers right away. Hang out at the table with us for a while. I guarantee you, within ten minutes your mom will ask me if I'm pregnant yet or when we're going to have a baby. That's when you step in."

"I step in. What do I step in?"

"You step up and answer her. You tell your mom we're not ready for children yet. You field all the follow-up questions. I will just smile adoringly at you and let you do all the talking. Do you think you can handle that?"

"Sure, I can do that. I'll just say, 'We're not ready to start a family yet.' Okay?"

"That's a good start, but it's probably not enough. You should add something else, like, 'We appreciate that you're interested, but we don't want to be asked about this. When the time comes, we will tell you when we're starting a family. Until then, let's talk about other things.' Like that. Otherwise they'll keep asking."

"You really put some thought into this, didn't you?"

"I did, because I'm tired of her meddling. I'm tired of answering her questions, and I am extremely happy that you will be taking care of it for me."

Relating While Autistic

"No problem. Like I said, I've got your back. Just one more thing," Justin looked slightly sheepish. "Would you write all that down for me? I don't want to leave anything out."

For Justin, learning that Maggie was uncomfortable about his mother's questions and having a script of what to say helped him to support her in the way that she needed.

Lucia & Naima

Lucia stared at the ceiling and sighed deeply. Three times. Finally Naima turned over towards her.

"Are you mad at me? Just because I'm too tired to make love tonight?"

"I'm not mad at you." Lucia sighed again. "I'm more hurt than mad. It feels like you don't love me anymore, not like when we first fell in love. Is this what being married is like? No more sex?"

Naima sat up and turned on the light. "No, of course not. You know better. But you can't expect me to automatically be in the mood every time you are. I had an exhausting day today, and I'm just not into it. Can't you accept that?"

"Of course, you have a right to say no. But it was the way you turned me down that hurts."

"Why, what did I say?" Naima really didn't remember, she had been so overstimulated by a long work day filled with social

Chapter 9: Big 3 Hot Topics: Families, Money, and Sex

obligations and meetings that when they got to the bedroom she just wanted to collapse into sleep.

"You said, 'Oh, hell, no!' is what you said. How am I supposed to take that?"

Naima covered her face. "I really said that? To you?"

"Exact words. Emblazoned on my wounded heart."

"That 'hell, no' wasn't about you, Lucia. It was about the day I just had. I've had so many meetings and it was so peopley all day that I just needed to be alone and not be touched." She put her hand on Lucia's. "It doesn't mean I don't love you, I just had nothing left for anyone or anything but sleep."

"I'm sorry you had such a rough day. I didn't realize. You didn't say anything."

"Well, I'm sorry I didn't say anything. Let's plan a romantic evening tomorrow night, how about that?"

"That would be perfect."

"But I'm still really sorry about the way I turned you down. Hearing you repeat back my harsh words to you felt like a slap in the face, so I can only imagine how it felt to you when I said that."

"Yeah, it was hard to hear, all right."

"I don't want to do that to you again." Naima squeezed Lucia's hand. "So, let's come up with a script."

"You want to write a script for how to say no to sex?"

"Yes, exactly. What would be the best way for you to hear a 'No' and realize it wasn't personal?"

Relating While Autistic

Lucia thought about it. "I guess, if you led with, 'I love you,' and followed up with the explanation of why you're not in the mood, it would help."

"Good idea," said Naima. "Maybe adding a plan for the future, too."

"Yes!" Lucia was on board now. "So, here's our new three-part script for taking a pass on a romantic pass: First, a statement of love. Second, a brief Why. Third, a proposition for the future. Does that work?"

"Absolutely." Naima was relieved that they had a plan. "Lucia, I want to tell you that I adore you, I am too overstimulated to be touched tonight, and I'd love to make love with you tomorrow night if you're in the mood."

"That sounds wonderful! But we should probably specify that the future date is also subject to either one of us needing to reschedule if we get overwhelmed and need to be alone."

"Absolutely, no pressure. Just one more thing." Naima yawned.

"Anything."

"I really need to sleep now. Good night, sweet dreams, and don't talk to me before the alarm goes off tomorrow."

For Lucia and Naima, it was important to have a script for how to lovingly and respectfully reject a sexual overture without hurting their beloved's feelings or damaging their relationship.

Chapter 9: Big 3 Hot Topics: Families, Money, and Sex

Crow & Daisy

CROW: Are you sure you need that fancy coffee?

DAISY: The spice must flow. Why else would I be standing in line in here? Just to chat up the barista?

CROW: It's just that we have coffee at home.

DAISY: I know, but 'tis the season for pumpkin spice espresso.

CROW: It's a lot cheaper to just make a cup of coffee at home.

DAISY: But this is pumpkin spice espresso.

CROW: The way they upsell and overcharge for basically hot water and bean grounds is a crime. You shouldn't support this nonsense.

DAISY: You may not have heard me. Pumpkin. Spice. Espresso.

CROW: And how much do they charge for frothing up the milk so it's mostly air? Are we buying air now?

DAISY: What is going on with you? You're not usually the uptight one in this dynamic duo.

CROW: So, are you the uptight one?

DAISY: There is no uptight one. That's why we are such a brilliant and magical couple. So why are you all over my case about my latte? Are you under an enchantment that turned you into a harpy all of a sudden?

CROW: I just don't want you wasting your money on stuff we could make at home. Money doesn't grow on trees, you know.

Relating While Autistic

DAISY: I cannot believe you just said that. Are you your father now? Don't you realize that money is made of paper? It literally grows on trees!

CROW: You know what I mean.

DAISY: Truly, I do not. I don't know who this is who has taken over Crow's body, but I command you, begone, foul spirit! I exorcise you! Out, out!

CROW: Stop, please. I just worry about money sometimes. Is that a crime?

DAISY: If worrying were a crime, most of the population of the world would be in jail right now. Worry all you want, but don't go sloshing your worry all over me. Do not come between me and my pumpkin spice!

CROW: How do I keep from worrying when I see you throwing away money on frivolous things?

DAISY: First, it's a latte, not a yacht. Second, it's my money. Mine. You need to back off. If I were spending the rent money on lottery tickets, you should definitely say something, but don't disrespect my pumpkin spice craving!

CROW: You're right. You are. I will try to keep my worries about money to myself rather than dumping on you. Later, can we have a financial planning meeting, though? I'll feel better if I know we have a budget.

DAISY: Yes, definitely. We will make a budget. Because we are grownups and that's what grownups do. Now, do you want me to buy you a pumpkin spice espresso?

CROW: Ew, no, gross!

DAISY: Peppermint mocha it is, then.

CROW: You know me so well.

For Daisy and Crow, setting a date to plan a budget now that they were living together was a smart idea. It helped Crow to worry less about money, so that they could enjoy their time together and their fancy coffees.

THEY SAY

Money makes the world go round, everyone says. We live relatively okay for our age and the current world economy. At points there are stressful times, and she will get overly worked up about it, and rightfully so. I tend to just try and reassure her that 1) it will all work out in the end, and 2) I can DoorDash a night or two to earn extra money to make up for any shortfall. It has always worked out so far, and I believe it always will.

— Thomas McDonald III

Relating While Autistic

Lucky for us, these three hot topics are not huge problems in our lives. The biggest one is probably children. Even though our children are adults, there can still be issues. When there's an issue with his children, the best thing I can do is stay out of it. We have a rule that he raises his kids and I raise mine. That works for us.

— Wendy B.

Chapter 10

Big Four Warning Lights

"An overall perceived negativity will quickly erode a relationship. And every successful marriage and relationship has, at its foundation, a deep and close friendship—partners who really know each other and are, at the heart of it, on the same side, part of the same team."

— Dr. John Gottman

Chapter 10: Big Four Warning Lights

If you want to have a happy, healthy, and long-lasting relationship, there are four big warning signs you should be wary of. Dr. John Gottman, whose extensive research focuses on divorce prediction and relationship stability, identifies four behaviors that are danger signs for couples. He calls them the Four Horsemen: Criticism, Contempt, Defensiveness, and Stonewalling. These big four warning lights may show up differently in neurodivergent couples. They may be misunderstood, and they may have different root causes.

When a person is a perfectionist, it can be difficult not to point out to others little improvements that could make their life better. Unfortunately, if the perfectionist's advice was not asked for, it can be unwanted, offensive, and be felt as Criticism. Whether or not the perfectionist intended to criticize their partner, that's how it can come across.

People with high moral and ethical standards who see others falling short may have little tolerance for people with different standards. Behavior can be seen as black and white, good or bad, with nothing in between. A person who would drop a scrap of paper on the ground might be seen as comparable to a factory polluting the ocean. Someone who would lie about loving a birthday present that they didn't like might lie about anything and can't be trusted. When someone expresses disapproval for people who don't meet their high expectations, it may look very much like Contempt.

Relating While Autistic

Some people have a history of being told they were wrong for being different and that they should change. As a child they may have been forced to engage in strict compliance behavior training. In school they may have been told they couldn't move their hands or bodies while learning because it might distract others. At work they may have been judged harshly for avoiding eye contact or handshakes. Perhaps they have been reprimanded again and again their whole lives, just for being themselves. It's no wonder that they're especially sensitive to any perceived criticism. It might look like Defensiveness, trying to deflect blame away from themselves, but if you look deeper and listen to their history, you may understand why they are on the defense.

Finally, another warning light which is particularly harmful to relationships is Stonewalling. Sometimes a person wants to coerce their partner into agreeing with them or giving in to their demands. If they don't get their way, they use the silent treatment or Stonewall them as punishment. The stonewalling partner withdraws, refuses to engage or respond, and acts as if their partner were invisible. This is particularly damaging to relationships.

On the other hand, if a partner is autistic, they may find that talking about emotionally charged topics is so difficult that they involuntarily shut down. Under extreme stress they may even lose their ability to speak altogether. As stress goes up, abilities tend to go down, so a normally talkative person may become nonverbal. They need time to process what they're hearing, and to think about their response. They may need to get away and regroup in solitude. This can look like Stonewalling, but it is not. Don't confuse someone who purposefully stonewalls their partner as a punishment with someone who experiences sensory or social overload and shuts down because of it. Give them time to recover and return to the discussion later, when they are able to communicate.

If you or your partner purposefully engage in any of these four harmful behaviors and this is an ongoing problem, it's important to seek help from a professional who is trained in couples counseling. The sooner you get help for these four warning lights, the sooner you can get your love story back on track.

RED LIGHT/GREEN LIGHT TIPS FOR PERFECTIONISM/ CRITICISM

 RED LIGHT: Every time you cut carrots for vegetable soup, your partner tells you that you should hold down four carrots together and cut them all at once to save time. They don't seem to hear you when you say that your hands are not strong enough to do it their way. You're tired of feeling criticized.

Relating While Autistic

 Green Lights:

- Do your best to control your reaction to their criticism. It won't help matters to lash out and get in an argument about carrots. It was never about the carrots, and an angry outburst is not helpful.

- Do find a time to talk about the issue. You know it's not good to keep your feelings bottled up, simmering with inner rage even as your soup simmers on the stove.

- Do wait until a time when you're both calm to bring it up, such as at a Family Meeting. Tell them how you feel when they keep repeating the same advice that doesn't work for you, and ask them to please stop.

- Do believe them if they say they weren't aware of how critical they were being and give them a chance to change the behavior. Because habits are hard to break, decide between the two of you what would be the best way to remind them if they forget. Making a joke of it can be a great tension-reliever, as long as the joke is not at anyone's expense.

- Do seek counseling if they won't listen or respect your feelings and if they continue to criticize you without trying to change. If your partner won't go to therapy with you, go by yourself. You're worth it.

Chapter 10: Big Four Warning Lights

 RED LIGHT/GREEN LIGHT TIPS
FOR HIGH STANDARDS/
CONTEMPT

 RED LIGHT: Your partner found out that when you do your taxes, you estimate how much you think you gave to charity, but you don't keep all the receipts to back it up. Since your income is not high and the likelihood that you'd be audited is low, you don't worry about it. However, since they found out they have been nagging you about it in a judgmental way. It feels like they are contemptuous of you, as if this one thing makes you a terrible person.

 Green Lights:

- Do talk it over calmly. Let them know how their attitude makes you feel. You may need to tell them the specific things they do or say that make you feel judged or as if they are contemptuous of you. Facial expressions associated with contempt include wrinkling the nose, and one side of the mouth is tightened or raised slightly, resulting in an asymmetrical expression. They might look in the mirror to try it and see what it looks and feels like, with feedback from you to let them know the expression you see in them.

Relating While Autistic

- Do cut them some slack if they are learning to match their facial expressions to their feelings. They may not be feeling as contemptuous as they look, so try not to judge them harshly for their reaction. Consider that ethics and morality are difficult subjects that many intelligent, good people disagree on.
- Do discuss the idea that a moral, ethical, good person may sometimes engage in practices that other people might see as immoral, unethical, or bad. That doesn't mean the person is bad, just that there are many gray areas. Talk about the issue that is distressing to them. Is it something you can agree to change? Or does it seem too petty and you are unwilling to bend over backwards to meet their expectations? Perhaps they could be in charge of gathering and saving charitable receipts for both of you, since it is more important to them than it is to you.
- Do pay attention to the frequency and degree of your partner's expressions of contempt. If this is a pattern in your relationship and talking about it does not decrease their contemptuous reactions to you, it is time to seek a counselor for the two of you or for you alone. No one deserves to live with contempt from their partner.

Chapter 10: Big Four Warning Lights

 RED LIGHT/GREEN LIGHT TIPS
FOR SENSITIVITY/
DEFENSIVENESS

 RED LIGHT: Your partner doesn't rinse the dishes before loading them in the dishwasher, and then when you put them away you find that they are not clean. When you point it out to them, they get defensive and emotional, and they blame the dishwasher for not doing a good enough job.

 Green Lights:

- Do think about how you let them know that the dishes are coming out still dirty. You might feel disgusted by finding "clean" dishes with food or grease stuck to them. You might feel frustrated with the need to rewash dishes that should have gotten clean the first time. Perhaps you're angry because this keeps happening again and again. Think about those feelings and how they might come across in your tone of voice and facial expression.

- Do choose a time to talk about the problem when those feelings are not fresh in your mind and on your face.

Relating While Autistic

- Do use "I" messages, and talk about how it affects you. "I feel frustrated when the dishes don't come out clean." "I like how clean the dishes come out of the dishwasher when they've been thoroughly rinsed before putting them in." Avoid accusatory "you" language, with words like "always" and "never," such as, "You never rinse the dishes properly," or "You always do it wrong!" Don't cheat on this by saying something like, "I feel that you never rinse the dishes properly. That's just "you" language dressed up like an "I" message.

- Do ask them to share what doing the dishes is like for them. There may be sensory reasons behind the way they do things. Do they hate the feeling of touching greasy dishes with food on them? That may be why they put them into the dishwasher immediately. One possible solution could be wearing household gloves to rinse the dishes. Another might be to switch chores, so that they are not the ones to put the dishes in, or that you work together, you rinse and hand them the dish, and they put it in the machine. Sharing a chore like this can be a good time for catching up on your days or talking about what movie you want to watch later.

- Do arrange a fair trade for the job you don't want to do. If your partner just takes over all the jobs that are

Chapter 10: Big Four Warning Lights

difficult for you, without you doing another job for them, it's not an equal partnership. It would send the message that you aren't capable, and set precedence for one person to do an unfair portion of the housework. Trade a chore you dislike that they tolerate for one that they dislike and you tolerate.

* Do remember that defensiveness often stems from feeling unsafe or less-than. Your partner may have a constant critic in the back of their mind telling them how terrible they are at doing things. When you tell them something is wrong about what they're trying to do, it can feel exaggerated because it's piled on top of their own negative self-talk. If this is your partner's reality, consider counseling to learn to reframe their negative self-talk and increase self-esteem. Be sure to find a counselor who is neurodiversity-affirming, someone your partner feels safe talking to.

RED LIGHT/GREEN LIGHT TIPS FOR SHUTTING DOWN/ STONEWALLING

RED LIGHT: Periodically your partner shuts down and stops talking to you. At all. They don't answer your questions, they don't talk about their day, nothing. You feel like you're living alone, even though there's another person living with you and even sleeping in the same bed, but not a word for days at a time.

 Green Lights:

- Do let them know, calmly, perhaps at a Family Meeting, that you notice they haven't been talking to you. Ask if they have a reason for this.
- Do listen to their answer, without assuming that you know their reason for not talking to you. It might not be about you at all.
- Do look at their Why. If their reason for giving you the silent treatment is that their job is stressful right now and they are all "talked out" before they get home, this is social or sensory overload and not actually stone-walling. Plan for the first hour or so after they come

Chapter 10: Big Four Warning Lights

home to be time spent alone, doing de-stressing activities. This might be playing a video game, or taking a nap or bath, or whatever is most relaxing and rejuvenating for your partner. Don't talk to them during this time, just give them lots of space. When they're ready to come out, keep the conversation low key and unemotional so that they don't get overwhelmed again. Consider whether this is a temporary part of their job that will get back to normal soon or whether they should think about asking for accommodations, job hunting for something less stressful, or seeking counseling or life coaching to develop more effective coping strategies.

Don't turn a blind eye to actual stonewalling. If their reason for not talking to you is that they are angry and this is their way of punishing or trying to manipulate you, this is stonewalling. It is damaging to your relationship and should not be ignored. Suggest couples therapy with someone trained in relationship counseling. If your partner won't go with you, go by yourself. Help is available. No one deserves to be punished by their partner.

Relating While Autistic

WHAT SHALL WE TALK ABOUT?

*Family Meeting Discussion Openers about
the Big Four Warning Lights*

Ask and answer any or all of these questions, taking turns with
your partner:

1. Has either of you felt unjustly criticized in your relationship?
   Was it a one-time thing or a pattern? What can you do to
   improve this situation?
2. Has either of you felt that you can't live up to your partner's high
   standards, and you feel unjustly judged or held in contempt?
   Does this happen often or only once or twice? What can be
   done to help change this?
3. Has either of you felt that whenever you bring up a touchy
   subject, your partner gets overly defensive and avoids the
   discussion? Is this a regular thing between you? What might
   help?
4. Has either of you felt stonewalled by your partner, like they
   were giving you the silent treatment? Could it have been an
   involuntary shutdown due to sensory or social overload rather
   than a punishment? How often does it happen, and can you
   predict the kinds of things that seem to set it off? If so, discuss
   how you can avoid those situations or provide accommodations to make them more manageable.

Chapter 10: Big Four Warning Lights

5. If any of the Big Four Warning Lights are common, repeated experiences in your relationship, seek help from a therapist specifically trained in couples counseling. You can work it out. If your partner won't go with you, go by yourself. You deserve to be treated respectfully.

DATE NIGHT THEME

Comfort Date

Choose somewhere familiar and cozy, such as your home. Decide that this will be an evening of comfort—comfort foods, comforting activities like watching an old favorite movie, comfortable clothes, and, most importantly, comfortable conversation. Declare this an evening free from the four horsemen.

Relating While Autistic

FICTIONAL COUPLES

Trish & Bill

"Did you remember to close the kitchen screen?" Trish called as she went to get ready for bed.

Bill put his hands over his face. "Why can't you get off my back about that? I said I was sorry. I don't know what you want from me. I'm just a terrible husband!"

Trish stopped and went back to him. She put her hands over his, and after a moment, she gently removed them so she could look at his face. "What's all this about? Why are you so defensive over a simple question?"

"I know you're still blaming me for the one time I forgot, and I just want to get past it. I feel bad enough already."

"Oh, I get it now. You're talking about the kitchen table incident."

"Of course I'm talking about the incident."

"Okay, I admit I was shocked to walk into the kitchen and find an animal on the table."

"Not just shocked, you screamed so loudly I thought you were badly hurt. It scared me to death. And then it turned out to be just a cat."

"Well, I didn't realize at first that it was just Leo from next door."

Chapter 10: Big Four Warning Lights

"And I know it was my fault for not fully closing the screen. I was careless, and now you can't forgive me. The kitchen table incident will be the end of us, and it's all on me if I lose you."

"You're not losing me. It was a simple mistake. Of course I can forgive you."

"But you can't stop reminding me about it over and over again. Every time you do, I realize you don't trust me. And it's not like I could have predicted Leo's ability to slide open a screen with his claws."

"Of course I still trust you. No one can predict what Leo might be capable of. He is the neighborhood enigma."

"But every time you bring it up, I relive the experience of hearing you scream and then discovering that I was the cause of it. It keeps replaying in my mind like a loop. I can't help being defensive about it."

"I didn't realize, Bill. I'm sorry. I thought I was just giving you a helpful tip, not opening up past wounds. I'll try to remember to stop reminding you about latching the screen every night. Will that help?"

"Thank you, yes. And I'll try not to get so defensive about it and get stuck in a negative loop."

"Are there any strategies you can think of that might help?"

"Yeah, I guess I should just tell myself, 'Stop,' every time I get into a spiraling thought trap, and then think about something different, something that I won't feel defensive about."

Relating While Autistic

"What about replaying a favorite scene from *Star Trek* in your mind whenever you get stuck, to keep your brain occupied with something you enjoy?"

"Great idea. You know me so well." Bill put his arms around Trish, and they hugged, not too tightly, not too lightly, the perfect hug. "Now, if you'll excuse me, I'm going to double-check that the kitchen screen is latched."

For Bill and Trish, communicating the reason for his defensiveness and coming up with a plan for the future made all the difference.

Justin & Maggie

Justin stood at the sink shaving while Maggie paced behind him, sighing loudly. Finally she stopped and turned toward Justin.

"You haven't even noticed, have you?" she demanded.

Justin stopped shaving. "Noticed what?"

"I haven't spoken to you in twenty-four hours. I've been giving you the silent treatment, and you didn't even notice."

"Oh, that. I guess I thought you were quieter than usual. I wasn't worried about it, though. I like quiet sometimes, too."

"I wasn't talking to you because I'm so mad at you. And you're doing it again."

"Doing what? Shaving?"

"Look in the sink, Justin. What do you see?"

Chapter 10: Big Four Warning Lights

Justin looked down. "Hairs. From my beard. Why?"

"So you are able to see the hairs."

"Sure, they're right there in the sink. But why are we talking about them?"

"Okay, so after you finish shaving, what do you do next?"

"I finish my morning routine, and then it's time for work."

"And what about the hairs in the sink?"

"What about them?"

"You just leave them all over the sink?"

"What difference does it make? They don't last long."

"What do you mean, they don't last long?

"They're always gone next time I'm in here. They don't last."

"Do you think hairs just melt, or dissolve into air?"

Justin looked at the hair and thought for a moment. "I guess that doesn't make sense. Hair doesn't melt. But it's always gone, so how do you explain that?"

Maggie glared at him and pointed to herself. "Me. I clean up your beard hairs."

"Why would you do that?"

"Because I need to use this sink, too, and a sink covered with hair is gross. So I've been cleaning up after you, thinking you just forgot, but you never do clean it up yourself. I'm sick of it, Justin."

Justin kept staring at the sink, feeling his face grow warm with embarrassment. "Wow. I'm ... so, you've been cleaning up after me?" he asked. "But what about before we lived together?"

"I'm guessing your mom cleaned it up for you. Moms do that."

"I'm so stupid. Why didn't you tell me?"

"Well, I've been giving you the silent treatment, waiting for you to notice that I'm upset and ask me what's wrong."

Justin chuckled. "I guess the silent treatment doesn't work on me. I figured, if you don't have anything to say, you don't have to say anything."

"Well, I guess I learned not to try using the silent treatment on you next time I'm upset. I'll just tell you how I feel."

"And I learned that I need to clean up my own messes."

Lucia & Naima

"I can't believe you left such a small tip! What kind of person stiffs their waitstaff?" Naima looked at the check in disgust.

"What do you mean, stiffed them? I left a tip."

"You call 10% a tip? That's an insult!"

"Wait a minute, I picked up the meal at curbside, no one had to bus a table for us." Lucia grabbed back the check. "I don't know why you're going off on me about a stupid tip."

"Stupid tip? Well, maybe you never had to wait tables to make a living. But most people appreciate how underpaid restaurant employees are, and they tip accordingly."

"It's not my fault if management refuses to pay them a living wage."

Chapter 10: Big Four Warning Lights

"It may not be your fault, but leaving a lousy 10% tip is a real jerk move. Any decent person would realize that under-tipping your server is not going to get the restaurant owners to pay them more."

"Wow. I can't believe this. Are you saying I'm not a decent person?"

"Well, I'm saying 10% is not the kind of tip a decent person leaves. It's messed up."

Lucia shut her eyes for a moment, took a deep breath, and then left the bag with their food on the table and went to the bedroom, closing the door behind her. Naima sat at the table and thought about their conversation.

Having worked her way through school as a waitress, Naima was sensitive about the injustices rampant within the food service industry. She always tipped at least 20%, and often 25%. Even if the service was subpar, she suspected that the server might have been having a bad day and left an even bigger tip. Maybe that person had just lost someone close to them but had to keep working through their grief or they'd risk losing their job. Who knew what invisible battles other people fought every day? Times were hard for a lot of people these days, and for Naima, leaving a generous tip was one way she could try to brighten someone else's day. This was not a small issue for her.

Relating While Autistic

But did that mean she had to come down so hard on Lucia? Thinking back over what she had said and how she had said it, Naima felt her cheeks grow warm. She was ashamed to admit to herself that she showed more empathy for a restaurant employee she'd never met than she did for her own wife. She owed Lucia an apology.

"Lucia? Can I come in?" Naima waited, not wanting to intrude before she knew Lucia was ready to talk to her. "I want to apologize for how I spoke to you."

After a pause, the door opened, and Lucia silently let her in.

"Lucia, I am so sorry. I didn't mean those things I said to you. You are the most decent human being I know. I don't know why I went off on you about how you tipped."

"Naima, I understand how deeply you feel about social injustice, and I love you for it. But I don't like feeling the way I do right now, as if you're looking down on me and viewing me with contempt. It feels horrible."

"I know, and I am so sorry. You don't deserve that. You bought dinner tonight, so the decision about tipping was yours. I shouldn't even have looked at the check, it's none of my business. I'm sorry."

"And I'm sorry if you feel like I treated the staff poorly. I just thought that since I ordered online, no one had to take my order at the table, and then I picked it up at the counter. It seemed like 10% was fair."

Chapter 10: Big Four Warning Lights

"And I guess I wasn't thinking about what's fair but what a difference a few extra dollars might mean to the people who served you, no matter how much or how little they did this time."

"Well, next time I'll leave a bigger tip, if for no other reason than to help make up for the next jerk who comes along and leaves a lousy 10%."

"I love you, Lucia, and I don't like myself when I treat you disrespectfully."

"It's not how we usually are when we're together. Let's promise to check our contempt at the door when we come home, and be our best selves when we're together."

"Agreed!"

Crow & Daisy

CROW: Are you sure you want to go to this party? It's going to be all work people, no one you know.

DAISY: Of course I want to go! I've never met anyone from your work. It'll be fun!

CROW: Well, the people I work with aren't like the guys from D&D. It's, you know, work.

DAISY: Hmm. So you're saying work is different from D&D. Astonishing. I'm flabbergasted. That's sarcasm, by the way.

CROW: Yes, I recognized the sarcasm. I just mean, they're not used to, well, people like you.

Relating While Autistic

DAISY: People like me?

CROW: I'm just saying, try to be less enthusiastic about every-thing. Be cool. Maybe, don't talk so much. Especially about D&D.

DAISY: Don't be my uncool self, is that what you're saying?

CROW: I have to work with these people, Daisy. My boss will be there. They only know my work persona, not my real self, and I don't want them to judge us. To judge me.

DAISY: Are you telling me that you spend all day at work pretending to be a normie? They don't know you're weird?

CROW: God, no. I want to keep this job. That's why I cover up my tats and take out most of my piercings for work. If you come to the party and you get hyper and start fluttering all over the place, they will form opinions. Negative ones. And it will reflect on me.

DAISY: Are you seriously telling me that you're embarrassed by me being myself? You want me to mask and pretend to be like the neuromajority? Is that what you're saying here, Crow?

CROW: Well, not usually, but this is different. If I bring a weird date to this party, they'll think I'm weird too. I'll get shut out and passed over for leadership roles. I'll be stuck in a dead-end job, or even lose my job.

DAISY: So, I'm so weird that if your boss meets me, you'll get fired? Is that what you're saying?

Chapter 10: Big Four Warning Lights

CROW: When you say it like that it sounds bad.

DAISY: It is bad. You're worse than my inner critic, and I didn't think that was possible. Don't worry, I'll stay home. I don't want to be around you right now, anyway.

CROW: Wait, Daisy. I'm sorry.

DAISY: I'm sorry, too. Sorry you're so ashamed of me.

CROW: This is going all wrong. It's not what I mean. Can we have a do-over?

DAISY: I don't know. Wouldn't a do-over be weird? I'm guessing your boss never takes a do-over.

CROW: Daisy, I'm terrified. A lot of people are getting laid off. I don't want to lose this job, but I also don't want to lose you.

DAISY: I had no idea you were worried about getting laid off.

CROW: It's because I'm so stoic and inscrutable. But inside I'm a quivering mass of anxiety. Sorry for slopping my messed-up paranoia all over your magnificence. You don't deserve that.

DAISY: True, I don't. So, what do we do? Do you want to go without me? I won't be mad.

CROW: Actually, no. I'll feel better if you're with me. But I'm still worried about being judged.

DAISY: You do realize I was a drama kid in school? I can act like a Normal Norma at the party.

CROW: You'd do that?

Relating While Autistic

DAISY: I'll give an Oscar-worthy performance. Here are my conditions: First, you make sure I get fed and hydrated. All my energy will be on my role, not on keeping my strength up.

CROW: Sure, I'll bring you refreshments. What else?

DAISY: We stay no longer than two hours. If I need to leave before the two hours are up, I'll give you a secret signal, and you get us out of there fast.

CROW: No problem. What's the signal?

DAISY: I'll start talking about the weather.

CROW: What if you just talk about the weather as a normal part of a conversation? How will I know if it's the signal?

DAISY: How often do I talk about the weather?

CROW: Oh, right.

DAISY: So, if I mention the weather, it's the signal, and we're out of there.

CROW: Got it. Anything else?

DAISY: Yes. This will be exhausting. Tomorrow, I will do nothing but lay about and maybe read, watch TV, or play a video game. I will not cook or do any other chore. You will be my minion and do all for me, out of your deep gratitude for the spectacular role I will play tonight.

CROW: As you wish, your majesty. Your slightest desire is my command.

DAISY: I think I could get used to this.

Chapter 10: Big Four Warning Lights

CROW: You know, this party is starting to almost sound like fun. I can't wait to see your performance.

DAISY: It will be dazzling, I assure you. By which I mean dazzlingly boring, beneath anyone's notice, a beautiful, soft-spoken wallflower.

CROW: Thank you for doing this. I'm sorry my anxiety got the better of me and that I was so critical of you. You're actually pretty great, exactly the way you are.

DAISY: I know, Crow. I love you too.

THEY SAY

In our relationship, we never do contempt, not ever! Not stonewalling either. Those things will kill your relationship. I can't say he's critical of me, either, and I don't believe I'm critical of him. Defensiveness, yes. I can be defensive if it has to do with my children or if I perceive (correctly or not) that he is criticizing me. I tend to get angry and then I shut down. He may also feel angry, so we take a little space until we can discuss the issue more positively. Ultimately, we seek resolution, so conflict is not something we are afraid of. It has taken me years of him being kind to trust him enough to get to this point. A side note: He's a staunch Republican and I'm more liberal. We disagree on politics,

Relating While Autistic

but our morals always align with one another. It helps that we've decided it is okay to agree to disagree, and if it is politics, we sometimes decide not to discuss it. If it's a fleeting issue that's sticky, the issue will pass. I am not going to risk my relationship to "be right." Trying to be right all the time can ruin a relationship. If it doesn't matter, it doesn't matter.

— Wendy B.

We have a ceasefire word—asymptote. In geometry, an asymptote is a line that continually approaches a given point but never reaches it. The meaning being: this conversation will go on like this forever without getting any closer to understanding. It's our nerdy way to say, "Let's stop this conversation." We would use this when we find ourselves continually talking past each other and getting too frustrated to see the other person's perspective. So, to opt out with no bad feelings, you just shout, "Asymptote! No more for now!"

— Jordyn

Chapter 11

Holidays, from Hazard to Happy

"The holidays stress people out so much. I suggest you keep it simple and try to have as much fun as you can."

— Giada De Laurentiis

Chapter 11: Holidays, from Hazard to Happy

olidays are loaded with high expectations. Everything must be perfect. Any couple might feel pressure during the holiday season, especially the winter holidays with their many traditions. Neurodivergent couples have the added stress of sensory and social overload. People with visual sensitivity might get migraines from flashing lights on a Christmas tree. The aroma of latkes frying in hot oil while the menorah candles burn can be overwhelming for someone who is sensitive to smells. Large indoor gatherings are stressful, even when there's no pandemic to worry about, if you have only a teaspoon of social tolerance and your partner has gallons. How do you navigate this precarious time and make it to the next year without falling apart? Here are some tips to keep you on track.

 RED LIGHT/GREEN LIGHT TIPS
FOR HOLIDAY SCHEDULING

 RED LIGHT: **Both sets of parents want you and your partner to attend every holiday gathering with them, but you can't be in two places at once.**

 Green Lights:

- Do let your families know that you love them and you love spending time with them but that you need to set boundaries so that you won't get overwhelmed.

Relating While Autistic

- Do avoid the appearance of a contest between the in-laws. Whether or not you love them all equally, the important thing is to treat them fairly.
- Do get creative with when and how you celebrate.
- Do be creative with dates, rather than being ruled by the calendar. A Christmas dinner tastes just as good on December 23rd or 26th as it does on the 25th.
- Do protect yourself and your partner. If there are toxic relationships in one or both of your families, you have the right to limit your time with them or to not see them at all. If you need to avoid an all-family celebration when you know a toxic person will be there, be sure to schedule times later to make small celebrations with the family members who are important to you and who do not treat you poorly. Small gatherings with your favorite people are better than large gatherings where you are forced to socialize with someone who has harmed you with no remorse or apology. Protect yourself and your family by distancing yourself when necessary.
- Do plan your exit strategy so you can leave a party before you get overstimulated.
- Do block out a day or more after the event for recovery. You deserve to take care of yourselves.

Chapter 11: Holidays, from Hazard to Happy

WHAT SHALL WE TALK ABOUT?

Family Meeting Discussion Openers about Holidays

Ask and answer any or all of these questions, taking turns with your partner:

1. What is your favorite holiday?
2. What specific holiday traditions are most important to you?
3. If you could get rid of one holiday, or one holiday tradition, and never celebrate it again, what would it be, and why?
4. If you could create a new holiday, what would it be? Create it together and plan to celebrate your new holiday every year.

DATE NIGHT THEME:

Valentine's Day in July

Some holidays are so stressful that it might be easier to just stay home. Valentine's Day is one that many people struggle with. There seems to be a requirement to be especially romantic whether you feel like it or not. You're supposed to go out to a fancy restaurant, but you know it will be hard to get a reservation, and once you get there it will be crowded.

Relating While Autistic

Why not ditch February 14th as Valentine's Day and choose your own? Maybe July 14th is your personal Valentine's Day, or whatever day you like. It's a good idea to call your favorite fancy restaurant and ask them their least busy time of year or day of the week, and make your reservation for that time. If you like exchanging flowers, candy, or cards with expressions of your love, you can do that any time you choose.

Do choose a specific date rather than leaving it open-ended so you don't forget to do the things your partner loves. Plan with your beloved when you want to celebrate your love and what you would like to do and to give each other. If you'd rather have strawberries instead of roses, or sunflowers instead of chocolates, declare your preference in advance. Getting exactly what each of you wants is more important than surprising each other. When your personal "Valentine's Day" rolls around every year, it will be yours, and yours alone.

FICTIONAL COUPLES

Trish & Bill

"Our first New Year's Eve as husband and wife!" Bill inhaled and felt his chest fill with pride and contentment. "How shall we celebrate?"

Chapter 11: Holidays, from Hazard to Happy

"I never used to celebrate New Year's when I was single," Trish said. "What do you usually do?"

"Well, I used to watch a marathon of the entire *Star Trek* series and switch over to watch the ball drop at midnight, with beer and chips." Bill smiled at the memory, then stopped smiling. "But we don't have to do that now that we're married," he quickly added.

"Why not?"

"Well, now that we're married, we should probably go to a fancy restaurant or night club, all dressed up, and toast each other with champagne. Then we'll kiss at the stroke of twelve."

"Should we?"

"Well, I imagine that's what couples do. What do you think?"

"I think I don't like kissing in public, or champagne, or staying up until midnight. I know you don't like wearing a tie, and neither of us enjoys a crowded restaurant. Let's have a celebration that's just for us."

"Brilliant!" Bill sighed in relief. "What will our private New Year's look like?"

"Well, my ideal New Year's Eve with my husband would include getting bundled up in front of the TV under one enormous, puffy duvet."

"I'll bring in the one from our bedroom. It's cozy."

"Lovely! Then we'll have all our favorite snacks and drinks close by so we don't have to get up when we get hungry."

"Perfect! I'd much rather toast the New Year with a beer rather than champagne."

"And I'd rather have juice, but something fancy."

"How about peach nectar, with just a splash of vodka?"

"Yum!"

"Can we still watch *Star Trek*?" Bill secretly crossed his fingers. "You won't get bored, will you?"

"I'm never bored cuddled up with you, Bill. If I read a book or do a sudoku or crossword while we watch, you won't be offended?"

"Not at all!" He was relieved that he wouldn't have to forgo his *Star Trek* tradition now that he was married.

"I'm just not sure about staying up until midnight. You know, since I had a problem staying up too late on the computer, I've been trying to stick to a regular sleep schedule by going to bed at 10:00 every night."

"Well, it's always midnight somewhere, isn't it? When it's 10:00 here, we can turn the channel and watch the midnight celebration in New Orleans, or Chicago. We'll watch their fireworks or ball drop or whatever they do. And we can ring in the New Year together!"

"We'll kiss when it's the stroke of midnight somewhere in the world."

And they did.

Chapter 11: Holidays, from Hazard to Happy

Justin & Maggie

"So, how do you want to handle the holidays, now that we're an official couple?" Maggie asked.

"Same as before, I guess. Why?"

"Because last year we ate two Thanksgiving dinners, plus we spent the first, fifth, and eighth nights of Hanukkah with my family, and the Caroling–Cookie Exchange, Christmas Eve, and Christmas Day with yours. It was a lot."

"You're right. It sounds exhausting. How did we do it?"

"We just pushed through every single thing our families invited us to, and then you were exhausted and completely out of it until February."

"Hm. I don't really remember much about that, but it doesn't sound like much fun."

"It wasn't fun. You were overwhelmed, and practically catatonic. We can't keep doing that."

"Agreed. So, what do we do, and what do we quit? And who tells our parents? Not It!"

"Hey, no fair. You can't call Not It! You're a grownup! You deal with your family, and I'll deal with mine."

"Okay, that makes sense. So, which things do we choose to break their hearts over?"

"Let's take one family at a time. If you had to choose to give up either Christmas Day, Christmas Eve, or the Christmas Caroling–Cookie Exchange party, which would you cut?"

Relating While Autistic

"Good question. The caroling and cookie party is early in the month and we get cookies, so let's keep that. But both Christmas Eve and Christmas Day is a lot going on all at once. Let's drop one of those."

"Okay, which one?"

"I think my parents would rather we spend Christmas Day with them, and we can skip Christmas Eve with the midnight candle-light service at church. The smell of all those candles bothers me anyway, especially mixed with everyone's perfume and the pine branches everywhere."

"Okay, that's smart. We'll skip Christmas Eve and spend a quiet night at home, to be ready for Christmas Day with your family."

"Your turn. Which night of Hanukkah do you want to skip?"

"The fifth night is special because that's when the majority of the candles have been lit. The light overcomes the darkness; it represents resilience and endurance. But, I really love the first and last nights with my family best. Let's cut the fifth-night celebration."

"Okay, as long as you're the one to tell them."

"Could we light a menorah at home, so I'll still get a fifth-night experience?"

"Of course! Whatever traditions are important to you, I'm there for it. But what about Thanksgiving? I don't think I can eat two complete dinners again."

Chapter 11: Holidays, from Hazard to Happy

"We're lucky our families live within driving distance. Let's alternate, dinner with one and dessert with the other, every other year. Fair?"

"More than fair. What a relief! I didn't realize I was dreading the holiday season until we started talking about it."

"Creating our own traditions as a couple is important. Even a family of two is a family."

Justin and Maggie had a much happier holiday season once they learned to say Yes to what was most important to them and say No to events that were important to others but not to them.

Lucia & Naima

"Surprise!" When Naima walked into the living room, Lucia turned off the light and lit one of the new candles she had bought.

"What's this?" Naima asked.

"It's a Mishumaa Sabaa," Lucia said. "As if you didn't know."

"Misha—what now?"

"You know, the Kwanzaa candles. It's the first night, so I lit the black candle for Unity."

Naima laughed. "Are you kidding me right now?"

Lucia's face fell. "Of course not. I'm honoring your holiday."

"Kwanzaa is not my holiday, it's made-up. I celebrate Christmas. You know that."

"But we can also celebrate Kwanzaa, can't we?"

Relating While Autistic

"I don't know anyone else who does. My grandma used to do a whole thing, but we were always trying to sneak out and hang with our friends. Once she passed we all kind of let it go."

"You let the seven principles go?"

"Of course not. We always talked about unity, self-determination, responsibility, purpose, all those things. The principles were core to who we were. But we didn't need a holiday for that. The whole seven-night celebration thing wasn't really part of my life after I was a kid. But it was sweet of you to think of this."

"I guess I should have asked you how you felt about Kwanzaa before I got the candles and the Kinara. Do you want me to take them back?"

"No, Lucia, don't do that. You went to all this trouble for me, decorated the table and everything. I am really touched." She looked at the placemat and corn display. "Actually, looking at all this reminds me of my grandma."

"Shall we keep it up, then?"

"Let's keep it. Maybe Kwanzaa will be a special time for the two of us, even if nobody else I know makes a big deal out of it. The meaning behind it is what's important. I love you for doing all this for me."

Celebrating a holiday from Naima's early childhood became a special time that the two of them shared every year, and she never forgot the love that Lucia put into planning that first Kwanzaa surprise.

Chapter 11: Holidays, from Hazard to Happy

Crow & Daisy

CROW: I hope you're not expecting me to make a big deal, now that we're living together.

DAISY: A big deal? Out of what?

CROW: You know, Valentine's Day. Last year I sent you those chocolates for your "Year of Something Tangible" because you asked for a birthday card, and I wanted to surprise you with something more.

DAISY: You astonished me! I loved it! Mushy cliches are so out of character for you, you caught me by surprise.

CROW: Well, I actually hate Valentine's Day, and I don't want you to expect me to make a big deal of it every year.

DAISY: You are such a romantic fool. So, I shouldn't expect anything for Valentine's Day ever again? Is that it?

CROW: Well, when you say it like that it sounds bad. But accurate.

DAISY: Look, I don't care about made up greeting card holidays, either. But I do care about you. I love you, and I know that you love me ... pausing for you to deny it ...

CROW: No, you got that right.

DAISY: Wow. Okay. So, we are in agreement that the two of us are head-over-heels crazy for each other, but we don't want The Man to tell us on what made-up holiday we have to admit it to each other.

CROW: It sounds like you want me to admit I love you on some other day, not February 14th.

Relating While Autistic

DAISY: That would be lovely, yes.

CROW: But isn't that the same thing? Only on a different day?

DAISY: Basically, yes. I will give you a pass on all traditional Valentine's Day expectations, but I do not excuse you from declaring your love for me, right out loud, with some semblance of regularity, on some other day or days. Days is better. Once a year is not enough.

CROW: Hm. Can I think about it?

DAISY: Of course. Take all the time you want. You have thirty seconds, and then the offer is off the table and we're back to heart-shaped boxes of chocolate every February 14th.

CROW: Thirty seconds? Is that all I get?

DAISY: Twenty-two seconds now. Tick, tick, tick…

CROW: I hate when people say, "Tick, tick, tick."

DAISY: I know. Time's up. Your answer?

CROW: Of course I'd rather show my love for you on any other day of the year. Are you happy?

DAISY: Almost always. Our agreement is now forged in the fire of my memory. From now on, February 14th means nothing in this household. Our love cannot be bound by the chains of commerce but must be free.

CROW: That's a relief. I do love you, you know.

DAISY: I know.

Chapter 11: Holidays, from Hazard to Happy

THEY SAY

After hating the holidays for years, we finally decided that we would carve out time specifically for the two of us to do something we enjoy and get some breathing space. We've been able to really keep good boundaries with our families about what we need so that we're not spending the whole holiday miserable, exhausted, and resenting them. It was scary to do at first, but our families were actually super receptive. They remembered what it was like for them being at the whims of family for holidays. The great thing is, while this is critical for ND folks, every couple and all families can benefit from approaching holidays this way.

— Tara, autistic woman, married to a man with ADHD

For holidays, we both enjoy short vacations and place them throughout the year if we can. For instance, we like to go to Rehobeth Beach, Delaware, and will spend one night and two days down there. We like to hit the beach on day one and eat at a good crab restaurant, then on day two a little more beach, the boardwalk, and then we're done with it all.

— Thomas McDonald, III

Relating While Autistic

This year we plan to introduce our children to one another at Christmas, and I am terrified! My children are also neurodivergent and nerdy, but his kids are strong, smart, sporty. I'm so afraid his kids will look down on me and mine. Here's what we are doing to make this work: First, we pre-ordered our holiday meal, so I don't have the stress of trying to cook everything as well as plan the menu, decorate the house, and do all the cleanup, all while wearing my nice Christmas dress. We have told the children what is on the menu and asked everyone to bring one dish to share. I have given a time limit on the family dinner Christmas Eve. We have decided to refuse some invitations, so I have time to regroup between functions. My goal is to be my best wherever we are; his goal is to help me so that the time we spend with others is enjoyable.

— Wendy B.

PART IV

ALL CLEAR!

Full Steam Ahead to Your Fabulous Future

"I look to the future, because that's where I'm going to spend the rest of my life."

— George Burns

"We've got this gift of love, but love is like a precious plant. You can't just accept it and leave it in the cupboard...You've got to keep watering it. You've got to really look after it and nurture it."

— John Lennon

Chapter 12

Stay On Track

"Love does not consist in gazing at each other, But in looking outward together in the same direction."

— Antoine de Saint-Exupéry

"It helps if you enter into a committed relationship prepared to work, ready to be humbled and willing to accept and even enjoy... bouncing between the poles of beautiful and horrible. "

— Michelle Obama

Chapter 12: Stay On Track

Your relationship is strong.

You've figured out how to change mixed signals into fixed signals by paying attention to both verbal and nonverbal communication, and by being aware of each other's social needs and boundaries.

You've learned how your beloved likes to give and receive messages of love, whether through words, touch, gifts, time, or actions.

You're careful not to get derailed when discussing the three big hot topics of family, money, and sex by listening respectfully to your partner with a heart for reaching understanding.

You skillfully avoid falling into the traps of the big four warning lights of criticism, contempt, defensiveness, and stone-walling.

Finally, you can just sit back and enjoy your loving relationship, with no thoughts or worries about the future, right?

Unfortunately, no. It's not that simple. Anything worthwhile is worth working on, and your relationship is no different. It will never be the right time to become complacent. Just because you have come to a place of joy, contentment, and understanding, don't stop working on communicating your love. Maintain focus on keeping your love strong. Fortunately, this can be an enjoyable, lifelong process.

Relating While Autistic

Date Nights should be non-negotiable. It doesn't matter if it's a quick trip to the grocery store with no kids in tow, a mid-day meet-up at a coffee shop, a fancy night at your favorite restaurant, a drive around the city, a walk around the block, or a trip back to the place you honeymooned. The important thing about Date Night is connecting, just the two of you, with no distractions. The frequency might be weekly or monthly, or whatever your schedules allow; just make sure you put it on your calendars in ink.

Making regular Family Meetings an ongoing part of your life is important. This is when you can synchronize your calendars and plan Date Nights. It's a good time to look to your future, whether that means preparing to grow your family, booking your next vacation, or planning for retirement. It's also a safe place to air minor grievances before they become big problems. Be sure that every Family Meeting starts and ends with something positive, whether it's expressions of love or your favorite snacks and drinks. Ending with a hug or kiss is also a good idea.

 ## RED LIGHT/GREEN LIGHT TIPS
FOR STAYING ON TRACK

 RED LIGHT: Your partner thinks Family Meetings is a stupid idea.

Chapter 12: Stay On Track

Green Lights:

- Do listen to their feelings about Family Meetings with respect.

- Do keep it low key rather than making the issue a big deal or blowing it out of proportion. Although you might think it's important for your relationship, whether or not you have Family Meetings is not a make-or-break issue.

- Do ask them what they don't like about Family Meetings, and what they find valuable. Your communication system is for the two of you to decide on together, and it won't be the same for every couple.

- Do remember that a couple who never has Family Meetings can still have a strong relationship. There are many ways to keep your communication lines open and to be supportive of one another in your own way and on your own schedule. Do what's right for the two of you.

- Do remember to plan something you will both look forward to after your meeting. Celebrate your love for one another.

Relating While Autistic

 RED LIGHT: You realize you haven't had a Date Night in months.

 Green Lights:

- Do pay attention. Date Nights are important, and you two deserve to carve out some time for yourselves out of your busy lives.

- Do take it in stride and don't worry that this means your relationship is in trouble. All couples have busy times when everything is hectic and it's hard to find time for each other. Relationships go through cycles, and if it's difficult to connect right now, remember the pendulum will swing back. Michelle Obama said about marriage, "You have to prepare yourself for long stretches of discord and discomfort." Don't give up when you reach those inevitable stretches. Your relationship is worth hanging in there until you get back to better times, as you will.

- Do put your next Date Night on your calendar, even if it will be a couple of months before you can fit it in. Knowing you have a special Date Night in your future will help you get through the hard times.

Chapter 12: Stay On Track

WHAT SHALL WE TALK ABOUT?

Family Meeting Discussion Openers about the Future

Ask and answer any or all of these questions, taking turns with your partner:

1. Looking ahead five years, what do you hope your lives will be like? Will your family grow? Where do you want to live? What about your work life?
2. What is one thing you could do today to help make those things come true?
3. What about ten years in the future? Twenty?
4. What do you love most about your life right now that you hope will always continue?

DATE NIGHT THEME:

A Year of Dates / Future Planning

Get out your calendars and pens (not pencils!) and schedule your Date Nights for the next year. Write them in ink, and treat them as if they were carved in stone. Of course emergencies can arise that cancel or postpone your plans, but make sure you agree on what qualifies as an emergency. Your relationship is worth prioritizing this commitment of your time, love, and devotion. You deserve it. Your beloved partner deserves it. So don't treat Date Night lightly; consider it as sacred and beautiful as your love.

FICTIONAL COUPLES

Trish & Bill

"Well, we made it through the holidays." Trish snuggled next to Bill on the couch. "I'm exhausted!"

"Me, too." Bill kissed the top of her head. "Let's just stay right here and not move a muscle until Easter."

Trish giggled. "That sounds heavenly." They sat in companionable silence for a while, and then Trish broke the silence. "Except..."

"Except what? Is something wrong?"

"No, nothing's wrong. I just realized we haven't had a Date Night since early October. I miss our special times."

"Well, let's get out our calendars." Bill slipped out of his wife's arms. "No, you just stay put, you're cozy. I'll bring both of our calendars and we can sync them."

When he returned, they opened up their calendars and started planning out their Date Nights for the year. For them, scheduling

Chapter 12: Stay On Track

two stay-at-home Date Nights, ordering take-out and watching a movie or playing a game together, for every one Date Night out at a restaurant or the movies seemed like the ideal balance. After they got them on their calendars, they decided to go through the year and plan themes for each one. Pairing a movie they would watch with food related to the movie theme was fun for them. Pinterest had a lot of good ideas for menus matched to movies but not many science fiction options, so they made up their own. It was so much fun, they decided to increase their at-home Date Nights and have fewer dates on the town. It suited them perfectly.

Justin & Maggie

"Tell me again, why do we have to have Family Meetings?" asked Justin. "It sounds so lame."

"Well, our relationship is important. I don't want to end up growing apart like my parents did."

"We're not your parents. And our relationship is important to me, too. But why Family Meetings? It makes me cringe just saying it."

"We know communication is vital to keeping love strong, and scheduling regular check-in times to make sure we're on the same page makes sense. What's your problem with it?"

"Well, the name, first off. 'Family Meeting' sounds like a joke. And I never know what to expect, but I assume you'll be telling me something I did wrong that I didn't even realize. It feels like being called into the principal's office."

"I didn't know you felt that way. Why didn't you ever bring it up at a Family Meeting?"

"Because if I bring anything up, the meeting will take longer. I just want to get out of there."

"Wow." Maggie took a moment. "Hmm. We definitely need to make some changes."

"Like getting rid of Family Meetings for good?"

"The thing is, we need to connect and communicate, but in a way that works for us. I don't want you to dread sitting down to talk with me."

"Uncertainty is the worst thing for me. When I don't know what to expect, I assume the worst."

"Okay. First, let's change the name. 'Family Meeting' was something I read about in a relationship blog, but we don't have to use it if you don't like it."

"I hate it."

"Got it. No more 'Family Meeting' then. What shall we call it when we plan to sit down and connect, synchronize calendars, and clear the air if needed?"

"I don't know. 'Check In' sounds like a hotel, and 'Check Up' sounds like a doctor's office." Justin gave it some more thought. "Well, we meet on Tuesdays. How about Tuesday Tune-Up? Too silly?"

Chapter 12: Stay On Track

"If it's not too silly for you, it's not too silly for me. I love alliteration. And it's not like anyone but the two of us will even know about it."

"Tuesday Tune-Up it is, then. But I still think I'll dread it. Different name, same thing."

"Since you hate anything unexpected, how about if we set an agenda ahead of time? We'll have some regular "Tune Up" questions we can both answer, and if either of us has a particular topic we want to bring up, we can let the other person know about it at least an hour before the meeting."

"I think you mean at least forty-eight hours before the meeting. I need time to get used to something."

"No problem. No new agenda items after Saturday, how about that?"

"Great. So, what regular questions did you have in mind?"

"I don't have anything thought out yet. What do you think?"

"Well, we want to check in and see how we're doing. How about asking the best and worst things that happened to each of us in the past week?"

"I love the idea of sharing the best thing that happened. But I don't know if I want to spend time thinking about what was the worst thing that happened. I'd rather get on with it."

"Okay, we won't go back over the worst parts of the week. How about this instead: First, what's the best thing that happened in your life since last Tuesday? Second, is there anything bothering you right now? Third, how can I help?"

"That sounds great. Anything else that would make it less objectionable?"

"Well, the guacamole is my favorite part. And TV after."

"Okay, we will have guacamole as long as avocados are in season, and we'll make something else we both like when we can't get good avocados."

"It's a deal. Thanks, Maggie."

"No problem. You were right about the name being lame, but I'm glad you're on board with the idea of keeping our relationship in tune."

Lucia & Naima

Lucia and Naima had been in book clubs before, and they loved having their own, private book club as a couple. They alternated reading or listening to a book about relationships with books just for fun, and they took turns choosing them. In January they laid out their book plans for the year. They loved reading, and having a special time set aside to have a glass of wine and talk about what they'd both read was a joy.

Chapter 12: Stay On Track

Crow & Daisy

CROW: I've been thinking.

DAISY: Like ya' do.

CROW: I've been thinking about our D&D characters.

DAISY: Ah, yes! Clever Galvorn, and Peridot Goldhammer the Mighty! (*Sighs*) I love us so much!

CROW: Same. We've been through a lot together.

DAISY: Oh, the skeletons we've slain, the orcs we've offed, the trolls we've trounced...

CROW: Not to mention the dragons we've decapitated.

DAISY: Such sweet memories!

CROW: I'm just saying, as much as our characters have braved, fighting side by side, I, uh, well, I think they might love each other. You know, like we do.

DAISY: Of course they love each other! How could they not?

CROW: Exactly. And when a chaotic-neutral half-elf cleric and a chaotic-good dwarf love each other very much, sometimes they—

DAISY: Gross!

CROW: —get married.

DAISY: Wait—what?

CROW: What did you think I was going to say?

DAISY: Never mind. You want our characters to get married in the campaign?

Relating While Autistic

CROW: Between battles, but, yeah. I think they'd be happy about it.

DAISY: Can a half-elf even marry a dwarf?

CROW: They can. Their children would be dwelves. But they don't have to have children.

DAISY: Children would definitely get in the way during a sword fight. But are you telling me you seriously want our characters to get married? How would they do that?

CROW: The Dungeon Master would officiate. He's cool with it.

DAISY: You already talked to Matt about this?

CROW: Well, like I said, I've been thinking about it for a while.

DAISY: Okay, what's the plan, then?

CROW: After the next battle, when we regroup back in town, Matt will have us gather at the plaza. Then Galvorn will propose to Peridot Goldhammer the Mighty—

DAISY: Or Peridot Goldhammer the Mighty will propose to Galvorn.

CROW: That works, too. So, then Matt marries Galvorn and Peridot Goldhammer the Mighty, and the entire band are the official witnesses.

DAISY: So, you were discussing all this secretly with Matt? And everyone else will be surprised?

CROW: Totally. What do you think?

DAISY: That. Is. AWESOME! We will blow them away! I'll bet

Chapter 12: Stay On Track

nothing like this has ever happened in the history of D&D, two characters getting married during the game! Brilliant!

CROW: (*Clearing their throat*) There's more.

DAISY: More? How can you top that?

CROW: Well, Matt is an ordained minister. He got some kind of online certificate, which sounds bogus, but is in fact legit. He can actually marry people. Humans. For real.

DAISY: Well, he doesn't need a certificate to marry Galvorn and Peridot Goldhammer the Mighty. They're fictional.

CROW: I know.

DAISY: So? Who cares if he can marry humans?

CROW: I do.

DAISY: ...

CROW: Daisy,

DAISY: Shut up!

CROW: I won't.

DAISY: Are you talking about, for real? You and me?

CROW: Yes. For real. You and me.

DAISY: Are you taking an arrow to the knee here? Seriously, if you kneel down and propose to me, I will puke.

CROW: If I were going to do that, I would have brought a bucket because we'd both be puking.

DAISY: That's not us, the whole proposal and bride and groom thing.

Relating While Autistic

CROW: No. That's way too "normal" for us. That's why...

DAISY: We get married during a D&D game, but for real? And no one knows it's real until afterward?

CROW: Matt has to know.

DAISY: We all know Matt can keep a secret.

They both chuckle and shake their heads, remembering all the hidden trap doors and giant spiders Matt kept secret until it was too late.

DAISY: You're really serious.

CROW: I am.

DAISY: Why?

CROW: I love you. I want to spend the rest of my life with you. I've always been afraid to think much about the future. But, if I know for sure that you and I will be together forever, then the future doesn't scare me.

DAISY: Aww, Crow! I feel the same way.

CROW: So, Daisy, will you marry me in the weirdest way we can possibly imagine?

DAISY: Try and stop me!

Daisy throws her arms around Crow, and they live happily and weirdly ever after.

Chapter 12: Stay On Track

THEY SAY

My Date Night advice is: no kids, and make plans for what your partner may like to eat. Think of something nice to end the night, like a quiet evening or a TV show binge. What I love the most about my wife, Laura, is she understands that I am different, but her love has always been 100%. She is the rock that holds everything together.

— Thomas McDonald, III

Kids are grown, so we don't have Family Meetings anymore. Our challenge is that my partner is very busy at work, so I have to wait for the appropriate time to bring up concerns or issues. I make lists of what's on my mind so that when he can give me his full attention I don't forget what was so important.

Oh, he's so lovely to me on our Date Nights! He's the perfect gentleman, opens my door for me. I like to put on a pretty dress and a little makeup, and he always compliments me. He asks me what I want to do, or he offers me suggestions. It's an "us" thing! I am part of the decision making, so if I am feeling casual it isn't a big deal. Sometimes we do things that are a big deal, like vacations or a fancy restaurant. He is always careful to give me plenty of heads-up so I can gear my head in that direction. If for some reason at the last minute I have a spin-out, he never makes

Relating While Autistic

me feel bad. Canceling plans last minute can mean you pay for the event anyway, and that sucks. But what's more important than forcing me to go somewhere is the value of his kindness and respect for my feelings. It's okay to stay home if that's what I need. I've never had a partner who was as patient, kind, and thoughtful as Chris. Knowing that he truly loves me, that he will not leave me, and that he values me as a whole person matters. He will never hurt me. We are each mature enough to apologize when we make mistakes, and to accept that apology when offered. Nothing matters more than the relationship. We put each other and our relationship first above all others—not including the children, of course. But whatever goes on in the world doesn't matter. Our love does. It takes effort and commitment, and he is so worth it! It's never a chore. It's a gift. I love him with all my heart, and I'll never leave him.

— Wendy B.

If Connie hadn't married me, I don't know what my life would have been like, or if I would even still be alive. It's not always easy to be married or easy to be autistic. Communication takes work. But easy isn't the most important thing. Our life may look different to other people, but it works for us. And it's worth working for. My life is better now because of Connie, and she says her life is better because of me. Being in love like this, having each other's backs,

Chapter 12: Stay On Track

knowing we'll be together for the long haul and not just when it's easy—that's a wonderful life.

— Martin, ND, married to Connie, NT

Acknowledgments

Many people have worked together to make this book a reality, and I am grateful to have them in my life.

My heartfelt gratitude goes out to:

My publishing family: Susan Thompson, Jennifer Gilpin Yacio, and all of the team at Future Horizons, Inc. It is a joy to work with you all, and I'm grateful to be on your team.

My family of birth, writers all: sisters Cynthia Whitcomb and Laura Whitcomb, brother Jonathan Whitcomb, and the memory of our parents David Whitcomb and Susanne Wise Whitcomb, who nurtured our love of books and writing.

My writing family: Susan Fletcher, Pamela Hill, Linda Leslie, Kristi Negri, Cherie Walters, who welcomed me into their author groups even before I had written my first book.

My readers: Cynthia Whitcomb, Siobhan Marsh, and sensitivity reader Cat Marsh. They made this book so much better.

My own dear family: my children Cat David Robinson Marsh, Siobhan Eleanor Wise Marsh, and Noel Maebh Whitcomb Marsh. They have reminded me that I could do this and encouraged me to give it my all even if it meant I wasn't always available on the home front.

And always and forever in memory and in my heart, their father David Scott Marsh, my own beloved.

Finally, I am so very grateful to the neurodivergent couples who shared their personal love stories for "They Say" so that others could be enlightened and encouraged by what they have already learned: Charlene & Scott, Jordyn, Marian, Martin & Connie, Tara, Thomas McDonald III, Wendy B. You have made a difference for all the couples who will read your stories. Thank you.

Resources

Chapman, Gary. *The 5 Love Languages: The Secret to Love that Lasts.* Northfield Publishing, 2014.

Gottman, John, and Julie Schwartz Gottman. *Eight Dates: Essential Conversations for a Lifetime of Love.* Workman Publishing Co., 2019.

Gottman, John, and Nan Silver. *The Seven Principles for Making Marriage Work.* Harmony, 2015.

Marsh, Wendela Whitcomb. *Dating While Autistic: Cut Through the Social Quagmire and Find Your Person,* the second in the *Adulting While Autistic* book series. Future Horizons, Inc., 2023.

Marsh, Wendela Whitcomb. *Independent While Autistic: Your Roadmap to Success,* the first in the *Adulting While Autistic* book series (Original title *Independent Living with Autism*). Future Horizons, Inc., 2019.

Mick Jackson, director, *Temple Grandin,* HBO, 2010.

Miserandino, Christine, Spoon Theory on "But You Don't Look Sick." https://www.butyoudontlooksick.com

Relating While Autistic

Schaber, Amythest @neurowonderful, *Ask an Autistic* on YouTube

Stimpunks Foundation: Mutual Aid and Human-Centered Learning for Neurodivergent and Disabled People. Source of the 5 Neurodivergent Love Languages.https://stimpunks.org